Trams in Eastern Europe

Michael Taplin and Michael Russell

Capital Transport

First Published 2003

ISBN 185414 273 9

Published by Capital Transport Publishing
38 Long Elmes, Harrow Weald, Middlesex

Printed by CS Graphics, Singapore

Ust Katav is a town in the Ural Mountains which has had a rolling stock factory beside the
hydro-electric plant underneath the Katav dam since 1899. From 1969 until 1991 about
14,500 trams were built here (650 a year) since then only some 1500 (125 a year). This view
is of the works test track.

Contents

Cover Photo **Probably the world's most successful tram, the ubiquitous Czech-built Tatra T3 and its derivatives is found throughout eastern Europe, with deliveries from 1961 to 1989. This coupled pair in the Czech city of Liberec (which is regauging from metre to standard) also show that advertising liveries are becoming common in this part of Europe.**

Frontispiece **The only east European country where the Tatra tram is almost unknown is Poland, which used its own Konstal factory in Chorzów to produce a standard design for all Polish sytems, the 105N. This pair are seen in Kraków.** *(Karel Hoorn)*

INTRODUCTION

Welcome to *Trams in Eastern Europe*, an illustrated introduction to the tramway and light rail systems in the eastern part of the continent, covering that part of the former Soviet Union lying west of the Ural mountains, and its former allied states in central Europe, from Archangel in the north to Yerevan in the south, from Plzen in the west to Zlatoust in the east. Capital Transport Publishing has also produced *Trams in Western Europe*, published in October 2002, and *Trams in Britain and Ireland*, published in June 2002.

The development of tramways in eastern Europe is inextricably bound up with the Soviet empire, which held sway over all the countries described in this book apart from Turkey (where there were no tramways until recently). All these states ran planned economies and were bound by trade agreements with the Soviet Union developed after the peace agreements of 1945. Some countries, such as Romania and Yugoslavia loosened such ties over the years, but the experience of Hungary in 1956 and Czechoslovakia in 1968 showed there was a limit beyond which Moscow was not prepared to go.

In general tramway development was encouraged as an effective way of providing mass transit when private car ownership was extremely limited. Once a city passed one million in population it became eligible for a metro, though resources for construction and operation were often a long time coming, and depended on local political 'clout'.

The brilliance of the Czech engineers in the Tatra company in developing the PCC design to mass production of a rugged and reliable tram was recognised in the decision that Tatra would be the major supplier of trams to COMECON countries, and up to 1000 cars/year left the Praha factory for all corners of the Soviet empire. Of course there were exceptions. Poland carefully copied two Tatras supplied to Warszawa and transferred production to its own Konstal plant. Romania tried to keep tramcar production internal (and even bought and copied a western-built articulated tram), but had to buy Tatras to cope with its tramway expansion programme (and the poor quality of its own product).

In the Soviet Union tram factories in Leningrad, Riga and Ust Katav met the balance of supply, but the trams they produced were rather crude by Tatra standards, and had a shorter working life in the harsh environment within which many systems operated. Nevertheless Soviet tramways succeeded in replacing their old two-axle trams in advance of many western countries by mass production and the planned economy.

All this came to an end in 1990 with the collapse of communism and the break-up of the Soviet Union. Suddenly undertakings had to find real money to buy Tatra trams instead of benefiting from some state bartered deal involving oil or potatoes. Very few had access to the necessary currency, and Tatra's market collapsed. After an unhappy decade, the assets are now part of Siemens' empire. The introduction of the market economy even meant that Soviet systems had to pay for trams from Ust Katav, which they were quite unable to do in the numbers required, since fares income was well below operating costs.

The re-unification of Germany provided something of a lifeline, as the huge investment in new trams for east German systems threw up lots of Tatras onto the second-hand market. Similarly the sweeping introduction of low-floor trams in west Germany meant many first generation 'modern' trams found their way east.

To some extent this is still happening, but now that western tram manufacture is in the hands of four multi-national companies, all eager to break into the eastern European market, the 'catalogue' trams such as the Alstom Citadis, Bombardier Cityrunner and Siemens Combino are starting to find their way to undertakings that can afford them. The accession of east European countries to the EU will increase this trend.

As the photos in this book show, 40 years of standardisation have left their mark on eastern European tramways, and the red Tatra or KTM-5 is a powerful symbol of that era. However the way that tramways have adapted and continue to operate today is worthy of study, while the environment they operate in provides plenty of interest, as Mike Russell's camera always finds out. Even he has not visited all the systems in European Russia yet, and we are grateful to the few 'local' enthusiasts known in the west for their assistance, particularly Aare Olander and Dr Sergei Tarkhov.

Travel in the parts of Europe described can be a challenge and adventure in itself, but can be done, either on an individual basis or through specialist agents. The tours organised by Thomas Fischer under the banner of the German Blickpunkt Strassenbahn magazine can be recommended.

Photography in eastern Europe is much easier than it has been in the past, though old habits can die hard amongst some locals. Difficulties can usually be resolved by adopting a friendly attitude and carrying a few postcards or pamphlets which show your interest in tramways. In general photography in the public domain should present no problems, but it is always wise to look at what might be in the background before raising a camera and avoid obviously military installations, and some industrial scenes may be considered taboo.

A narrow-gauge line connects the rail station at Trencianska Tepla with the town of Trencianska Teplice in Slovakia.

The Tatra KT4 four-axle articulated car was delivered to metre-gauge tramways in the former Soviet Union. Tallinn in Estonia has fitted a couple with low-floor centre sections from the German firm MGB, to increase accessibility. *(Karel Hoorn)*

In this book each system is headed as follows:

Town or city name *Opening year and track gauge* ***System length***

Some places have anglicised spellings which may be more familiar to some readers, and these are given in brackets in the headings. The opening year is the year that the first tramway was opened, regardless of mode of traction or subsequent replacement of a narrow-gauge system by a 'new' standard-gauge one. However for systems built new after a break of many years, the date of the new system is shown. The track gauge is expressed in millimetres: standard gauge is nominally 1435 mm, but small differences are found. The system length is the sum of the single measurement of each section of line (single or double track). Official statistics often represent the sum of each individual route length, which inflates the size of the system. We have tried to be thorough.

The rolling stock data is not intended to be a detailed fleet list (apart from some small systems where this is unavoidable). Only the main batches of cars in regular service are shown, and indication of a complete number series does not necessarily mean that the batch is complete. Many older cars, and individual new cars, will have been withdrawn. Many former Soviet systems have a fleet numbering system with the first digit acting a depot allocation code, which makes listing batches of trams in the conventional way impossible (and numbers on individual trams change as they are reallocated between depots); in these cases just outline details are given. Odd cars kept for works or special duties, and museum cars, are not shown. Those requiring detailed fleet lists are referred to the bibliography in the appendix. Rolling stock details shown are:

Fleet numbers *Car type* *Year(s) built* ***Builder*** *Notes*

Car types: A = Articulated, M = Motor Tram, B = Trailer Car, number = number of axles or wheel pairs.

Gloucester, July 2003   Michael R. Taplin
Photography (unless otherwise shown)   Michael J. Russell

ARMENIA

This ancient land-locked state has suffered from conflicts and natural disasters throughout its history, and has been at war with Azerbaijan since the collapse of the Soviet Union, with severe economic consequences. Nearly 50% of the population lives in the capital city, where the Russian-built metro is the only fixed-track public transport system with any future.

YEREVAN   1933   524mm   22 km

The capital of Armenia is situated close to the Turkish border and has been subject to many earthquakes over the years, which have disrupted infrastructure. A narrow-gauge horse tramway operated from 1906–18, but electric trams did not arrive until 1933. It is a hilly city that has seen considerable tramway abandonment over recent years, particularly since the metro was opened in 1981. Another tram route was closed in June 2003. Today one long tram route survives, linking northern and western suburbs, compared with six routes in 1995 and there has been no investment since independence from the Soviet Union. The future of the system is bleak therefore. Trolleybuses have been operated since 1949.

Rolling stock

004–111	M4	1983–87	Riga RVZ-6	Probably withdrawn
020–110	M4	1980–86	UKVZ KTM-5	About 40 remain

Advertising liveries have become quite common on former Soviet tramways, as exemplified by this Yerevan RVZ-6.

AZERBAIJAN

Sandwiched between Russia and Iran, the transition from a planned to a market economy since the collapse of the Soviet Union has been possible only through rich oil and mineral deposits and despite extensive conflicts. There has been no investment in public transport systems and it is uncertain whether there will be any tramway operation in the country for much longer.

BAKU   1889   1524mm   9 km

This port city on the Caspian sea is the national capital and a major centre of the oil industry, with pollution a major problem. The tramway system has been shrinking rapidly due to the complete lack of investment, but the remaining route is being operated by trams that have received at least cosmetic refurbishment, and may survive for some months. The city has a two-line metro, with the first section opened in 1967. A trolleybus system has operated since 1941.

Rolling stock

494–538	M4	1985–87	Riga RVZ-6	About 6 remain
490–556	M4	1985–87	UKVZ KTM-5	About 30 remain

This photo of a KTM-5 trams shows all the reasons why the closure of the Baku tramway is imminent.

One of the few operational Sumqayit trams lurches into the terminus by the Caspian Sea.

SUMQAYIT	1959	1524mm	10.5 km

Sumqayit (Sumgait) is a small city on the Caspian Sea near Baku that built a tramway to link the old central area with new industrial areas to the west. The economic situation since the break-up of the Soviet Union saw the undertaking heavily in debt by 1999, when its power supply was cut off. Thieves then stole the overhead wire, precluding a resumption of operation for many months. Visitors in 2003 found the tramway operational again with a limited service, but the system seems unlikely to have a long-term future. A trolleybus line opened in 1961, and has also seen periods of suspended operation.

Rolling stock
60, 63, 66–68	M4	1985–87	UKVZ KTM-5

BELARUS

Formerly Belorussia (White Russia), Belarus has traded lands with Lithuania and Poland during conflicts over the years. Despite a rather dubious political history since independence in 1991, the economy is flourishing. Most of the population are Russian though the Belarus rouble is no longer at par with the Russian one (the latter having been devalued). Two new tramways were built in the later years of the Soviet Union to support industrialisation. A local rolling stock building capability is being nurtured, but second-hand trams from Germany have also arrived.

MINSK   1892   1524mm   34 km

The capital of Belarus is a modern industrial city, restored after wartime destruction. The tramway system has reduced due to the construction of a two-line metro (first section opened 1984) but, has been stable in recent years. However planned extensions seem unlikely to materialise. There is a large trolleybus system, with the first line opened in 1952. The local AKSM factory, which builds trolleybuses, has also developed a modern tram design, which has entered service in limited numbers, and a prototype articulated car. However the opportunity of good-quality second-hand trams from Karlsruhe in Germany seems to prove more affordable, despite the problem of regauging, and more are likely to follow.

Rolling stock

001–025	M4	Tatra T3M	1991–96	
022	AM8	Tatra KT8	1994	
026–038	M4	AKSM 1M	2000–03	
031	AM6	AKSM 743	2001	
178–181	AM8	DWM	1969	Ex-Karlsruhe
369–513	M4	Riga RVZ-6	1979–88	

MASYR (MOZYR)   1988   1524mm   22 km

This tramway was built by the local oil refinery to provide cross-country transport for its workers from the small town residential areas. The line is built to light rail standards on private right-of-way and is still owned and operated by the refinery company, with a good standard of maintenance. Standard trams operate as coupled sets. The depot is beyond the northern terminus.

Rolling stock

001–047	M4	UKVZ KTM-5	1987–88

Opposite above **Minsk has modernised some of its RVZ-6 trams with new bodies and livery.**

Opposite below **The modern tramway in Masyr still operates its original KTM-5 cars.**
(Olaf Güttler)

A coupled set of KTM-5 trams on the 1974 light rail line in Navapolatsk.

NAVAPOLATSK   1974   1524mm   11 km

Navapolatsk is a new town dating from 1958 as a model city for workers. Another tramway built to fulfil the needs of the local oil and petrochemical industry, the system is owned and operated by the Polimir company to link residential areas with the factory/industrial areas. Private right-of-way permits high speed operation of the standard trams in coupled pairs.

Rolling stock
001–049   M4   UKVZ KTM-5   1973–92

VITSYEBSK   1898   1524mm   35.5 km

This ancient trading centre on the West Dvina River, formerly Vitebsk, had a Belgian-built metre-gauge tramway that was regauged in the mid-1930s, and badly damaged in the Second World War, with no operation in 1941–47. It is a traditional Russian system with street track in the city centre and reservation in the residential suburbs. There are two river crossings for trams. The system appears to be stable, despite the expansion of trolleybus operation, and the modern fleet is well maintained. Extensions are planned. Trolleybuses have been operated since 1978.

Rolling stock

260–299	M4	Riga RVZ-6	1974–83
310–399	M4	UKVZ KTM-5	1976–91
400–424	M4	Riga RVZ-6	1984–88
500–511	M4	UKVZ KTM-5	1991
512–517	M4	UKVZ KTM-8	1995–98

A coupled set of smartly turned out RVZ-6 trams cross the Dvina river in Vitsyebsk.

BOSNIA-HERCEGOVINA

This new state, created from part of the former Yugoslavia, still maintains the integrity of its frontiers through a strong UN force presence, but the shattered city of Sarajevo has returned to normal, and can now be visited by tourists safely.

SARAJEVO   1895   1435mm   16 km

The standard-gauge tramway was opened in 1960 to replace a narrow-gauge system, and includes a street loop around the historic central area, plus a branch to the railway station and a long interurban line running west to the suburb of Ilidza on reserved track. The Washington PCCs brought in to open the system were all replaced (one is preserved) by Tatras before the civil war, which saw the suspension of operation in 1992–94. Regular service was gradually extended to the whole of the system, while damaged trams were repaired and returned to service, and donated cars from elsewhere in Europe arrived to replace destroyed stock. Now the Tatras are gradually being rebodied and re-equipped to more modern standards, but it seems unlikely that money for new low-floor cars can be found at present. A trolleybus system is also operated.

Rolling stock

201–290	AM6	1973–83	Tatra K2	About 60 survive, some rebuilt
291–292	AM6	1969–70	Tatra K2	Ex-Bratislava
300–302	AM8	1986–87	Tatra KT8	Ex-Kosice
400–412	M4	1956–57	SGP	Ex-Wien, Most withdrawn
500	AM6	1974	Tatra K2	Ex-Bratislava, modernised
4000–4012	B4	1958–59	SGP	Ex-Wien, Most withdrawn

Memories of the Balkan war and subsequent aid for Sarajevo are evident in this view of a Tatra K2 tram.

BULGARIA

This former communist state has always been rather isolated, both economically and in terms of tourism, and has struggled to adapt to the market economy. The capital city has the only tramway system, which is being modernised slowly as funding is concentrated on the metro, but a large-scale switch to electric traction in other urban areas was achieved by the use of trolleybuses.

SOFIA   1901   1009/1435mm   182 km

The Bulgarian capital is a large and expanding city, with many new suburbs surrounding the older built-up area. The extensive tramway is the backbone of the city transport system operated by the municipality, although a Russian-style metro has finally started carrying passengers, and is being slowly extended. The central area features largely street track, but west of the railway station there is a complex of tram subways adjacent to a large depot. The traditional interurban line to Knayezhevo in the south-west was built on reserved track. There are also attractive private right-of-way sections uphill through the woods to Pl. Zavera in the south. In the eastern suburbs the narrow-gauge tramway has been

A self-built narrow-gauge eight-axle tram in Sofia city centre is followed by the more modern version of the local design.

replaced by a new standard-gauge line, opened in 1987, and subsequently extended to the city centre. Plans for further gauge conversions seem to have been postponed for economic reasons. Sofia has built the majority of its tram fleet in its own workshops throughout the post-war period, and developed its own design of articulated car, produced in six and eight-axle variants. Experiments with a convertible-gauge version for use on the new standard-gauge lines were not very successful, and the undertaking turned to the Czech supplier Tatra for both standard and narrow-gauge trams for a while. The economic turmoil associated with the fall of communism saw a change to reliance on second-hand trams from western Europe, including Duewag cars from Bonn and Tatras from Halle. The workshops are now busy rebodying their home-built articulated cars and a batch has been fitted with low-floor centre sections.

Unable to build enough of its own trams for the new standard gauge lines, Sofia saw the opportunity to buy the redundant Bonn tram fleet.

Sofia's newest narrow-gauge trams are these Tatras, operating in sets on route 5.

Rolling stock

101–211	AM8	1973–80	Sofia	
301–327	AM8	1977–78	Sofia	
400–467	AM6	1979–85	Sofia	
501–502	AM6	1985	Sofia	
503–504	AM6	1988	Sofia	
601–675	AM6	1968–71	Sofia	
701–725	AM6	1985	Sofia	
726–729	AM6	1986	Sofia	
730–799	AM8	1971–73	Sofia	
801–825	AM6	1985–86	Sofia	
826–827	AM6	1990	Sofia	
828–831	AM6	1987–88	Sofia	
832–850	AM6	1990–91	Sofia	
875–899	AM6	1969–71	Sofia	
900–915	AM8	1991(98–99)	Sofia	
916–937	AM8	1980(00–01)	Sofia	Low-floor centre sections
997–1130	M4	1976–81	Tatra T3	20 ex-Halle trams
2001–2040	M4	1991	Tatra T6	
2041–2058	M4	1998	Tatra T6	
4001–4033*	AM6	1986	Sofia	
4101–4137*	M4	1989–91	Tatra T6	
4138–4147*	M4	2000	Tatra T6	
4231–4244*	M4	1957–60	Düwag Ex-Bonn	
4401–4415*	AM8	1960–69	Düwag Ex-Bonn	

* Standard gauge

CROATIA

The first part of the former Yugoslavia to break away to independence, the eastern part was affected by the 1990s conflict, with boundaries still the subject of dispute, requiring the presence of a UN force in towns such as Osijek. Tourist travel can now be undertaken normally.

OSIJEK   1884   1000mm   12 km

Osijek saw fierce fighting during the civil war, and tramway operation ceased during the fighting, with damage to rolling stock and infrastructure. Life in this industrial town has now returned to normal and the tramway provides service on an east–west line into the suburbs, with a large loop in the well-preserved central area linking this to the railway station. Street track, including gutter-running segments predominates, though there is some reservation. The tram fleet was modernised before the conflict by the importing of Tatras from Czechoslovakia, including trailers for peak service. The shortage created by the destruction was overcome by the arrival of some Duewag articulated trams from Germany.

Rolling stock

6801–6810	M4	1968	Tatra T4	Some destroyed
7211–7222	M4	1972	Tatra T4	Some destroyed
8201–8204	B4	1982	Tatra B4	
8223–8226	M4	1982	Tatra T4	
9527–9531	AM6	1960–62	Duewag	Ex-Mannheim

The main street of Osijek is reserved for trams and pedestrians.

ZAGREB   1891   1000mm   49 km

The Croatian capital was physically unaffected by the civil war, but the consequences hindered economic progress for some years. Now the tramway is expanding again. Recent growth has seen expanding suburbs, particularly south of the river Sava. The tramway system runs on street track in the city, with some traditional gutter-running retained. Reserved track is common outside the centre. After a period of buying traditional rolling stock from Yugoslav builder Duro Dakovic, the undertaking switched to the purchase of Czech trams from CKD-Tatra, before a home-grown articulated car was developed. Second-hand trams from Germany helped it through hard times. Now the first batch of low-floor trams is due for delivery from a local consortium.

Rolling stock

101–163	M2	1957–66	Duro Dakovic	40 cars
164–171	M2	1961	Duro Dakovic	Ex-Osijek
203–229	M4	1974/75	Duro Dakovic	
301–351	AM4	1985/86	Tatra KT4	
401–429	M4	1976	Tatra T4	
431–485	M4	1979	Tatra T4	
486–494	M4	1983	Tatra T4	
592–697	B4	1954–66	Duro Dakovic	43 cars
701–730	B4	1974–75	Duro Dakovic	
731–742	B4	1969	Duro Dakovic	Ex-Beograd
801–830	B4	1975	Tatra B4	
831–885	B4	1979	Tatra B4	
900	AM6	1990	Duro Dakovic	
901–933	AM6	1960–64	Duewag	Ex-Mannheim
941–945	AM6	1967	Duewag	Ex-Mannheim
2101	AM8	1994	Koncar	
2102–2116	AM8	1997–98	Koncar	
(70)	AM6	2003–05	Koncar/TVZ	On order; low-floor

A two-axle tram with bogie trailer passes one of the latest articulated trams on a recent extension in Zagreb.

CZECH REPUBLIC

The former Czechoslovakia was the hub of tramcar modernisation for communist Eastern Europe, with its Tatra factory in Prague turning out up to 1000 new cars each year, based on a bogie tram built using American PCC licences. In addition to its exports, Tatra re-equipped all the Czech systems. The demise of communism and the introduction of a market-based economy saw a collapse of sales, just at a time when a large new factory at Prague-Zlicin had been completed to increase production. After a series of unsuccessful re-organisations the assets of the company were finally purchased by Siemens, but there seems little prospect of a resumption of large-scale tram production. In the meantime the rival company Skoda designed and built a new design of articulated tram (the Astra) which has achieved some success with Czech systems, as well as being exported to Portland and Tacoma in the USA. The larger Czech cities all have modern tramway systems in municipal ownership, and this tradition is likely to continue. Various companies are modernising the Tatra product pending the resumption of orders for new cars.

BRNO   1869   1435mm   79 km

Brno is an important commercial and industrial city at the centre of the former Czechoslovakia, and is well known for its trade fairs. Although many old buildings remain in the centre, it is a modern city with expanding suburbs. The tramway system has always been at the forefront of developments and upgrading to light rail standards started in the 1960s. All extensions built since then have been on reservation. There is street track in the city centre, including a pedestrian precinct. Further extensions are planned, but funding is tight. Like all Czech cities, the fleet was standardised on Tatra trams, and includes the latest KT8 articulated cars, some with a low-floor centre section. The K2 trams are one of the largest fleets of this type left in operation. A large collection of museum trams from Czech systems has been assembled at the former Lisen depot in the eastern suburbs.

Rolling stock

1023–1117	AM6	1973–77	Tatra K2	
1118–1132	AM6	1982/83	Tatra K2	
1201–1220	M4	1995	Tatra T3	
1495–1510	M4	1963	Tatra T3	
1511–1580	M4	1966–68	Tatra T3	
1589–1603	M4	1972	Tatra T3	
1604–1652	M4	1985–89	Tatra T3	
1653–1657	M4	1965–66	Tatra T3	Ex-Praha
1658	M4	1967	Tatra T3	Ex-Bratislava
1659–1668	M4	1997	Tatra T3	
1669–1670	M4	1992	Tatra T3M	Built for Samara (RU)
1701–1702	AM8	1986	Tatra KT8	
1703–1723	AM8	1989/90	Tatra KT8	
1724–1728	AM8	1993	Tatra KT8	
1729–1735	AM8	2000	Tatra KT8	Low-floor centre sections
1736–1737	AM8	1991	Tatra KY8	Ex-Kosice
1801–1804	AM6	1997	Tatra RT6N	Low-floor prototypes
1805–1819	AM4	2003	Skoda Astra	Low-floor

The Czech second city of Brno has modernised some of its Tatra K2 trams with new bodies from Pars Sumperk.

Brno is unique in operating the Tatra KT8 design with a low-floor centre section.

LIBEREC   1897   1000/1435mm   17.7 km

This town in northern Bohemia lies in the once disputed territory of the Sudetenland. The compact centre is built on a steep hill and its narrow streets have changed little over the years. A long tram route links the straggling suburbs and operates through semi-rural scenery in places, with a mixture of street track and reservation. The metre-gauge line has been re-gauged to standard in stages over recent years, and the project will be completed at its southern end in 2005. An interurban tramway, built in 1955, connects Liberec with the adjacent town of Jablonec, running through fine scenery with much private right-of-way. This remains a metre-gauge operation, but is scheduled to be replaced within five years by a regional tram operation using mostly the railway tracks between the two towns (but with rolling stock capable of street operation). Single-track sections with passing loop are found on both lines. Some trams from the metre-gauge fleet have been re-gauged and some standard-gauge trams brought in from other systems. The T2 trams are the last left in service anywhere.

Rolling stock

20–27	M4	1961–62	Tatra T2	Ex-Ostrava T2; 22–7 metre gauge
33/4/9–40	M4	1962–64	Tatra T3	Ex-Praha
35, 41/2/5	M4	1983–84	Tatra T3	Ex-Most
36–37	M4	1973	Tatra T3	Metre gauge
49–81	M4	1983–87	Tatra T3	
50–64	M4	1983–87	Tatra T3	Metre-gauge
82–83	M4	1963	Tatra T3	Ex-Praha
85	AM6	1996	Tatra RT6N	Low-floor

The last Tatra T2 trams are in service in Liberec. This pair is on the metre-gauge route 11 from Jablonec.

MOST   1901   1435mm   17.8 km

This town in the most heavily-industrialised area of northern Bohemia has been completely relocated since 1975 due to the spread of open-cast coal mining, and the new town is south of the old. The former metre-gauge tramway system was replaced from 1957 by a modern standard-gauge system on different alignments linking Most (since relocated as Novy Most) with the adjacent town of Litvinov. The last metre-gauge tram ran in 1961. Most of the system is on reserved track or private right-of-way and built to light rail standards, but there is some street track in Litvinov. The system was often used for trials of new Tatra tram designs, and demonstrators became part of the fleet when they were no longer needed.

Rolling stock

201–202	AM4	2001–2	Skoda Astra	Low-floor, ordered by Plzen
203–219/63/5	M4	1968–76	Tatra T3	
204–286	M4	1982–85	Tatra T3	
300–313	M4	1987	Tatra T3	Some are rebodied T1/T2

Industrial landscapes are a feature of Most, with its segregated tramway.

A Skoda Astra low-floor tram passes a Tatra T3 in Olomouc.

OLOMOUC   1899   1435mm   18.4 km

This Moravian town has changed little over the years, with many old buildings in the central area and a mixture of residential suburbs. The tramway system serves the main traffic arteries, mostly on street track, but with some reservation in outer areas, including single track on the Neredin line. Unusually for a small system, it features a grand union junction in the city centre. Expansion of the system has long been planned, but awaits better economic times. The standard Tatra fleet has been partly modernised and new low-floor cars have arrived.

Rolling stock

126/29/30	M4	1967–68	Tatra T3	
134–145	M4	1970	Tatra T3	
146–184	M4	1983–87	Tatra T3	
201–204	JM4	1999–2000	Skoda Astra	Low floor

OSTRAVA   1894   1435mm   59.5 km

The industrial conurbation of northern Moravia is centred on Ostrava, but extends to surrounding towns. Four transport undertakings were merged in 1953 to form the municipal operation which has developed the standard-gauge tramway network to replace the former narrow-gauge lines that once linked communities. The modern system features a high degree of reservation or private right-of-way, including an interurban line to the west that is single track with passing loops. There is some street track in the old city centre. After building up a fleet of standardised Tatra trams, the undertaking took delivery of Skoda low-floor cars. More recently, prompted by a contractual dispute, the undertaking's Martinov workshops has formed a partnership with the original designers of that car, Inekon, to build a similar design, now being marketed.

Rolling stock

721–748	M4	1966–68	Tatra T3	
748–772	M4	1970–73	Tatra T3	
773–798	M4	1976	Tatra T3	
799	M4	1966	Tatra T3	Ex-Praha
802–809	AM6	1966–69	Tatra K2	
810–811	AM6	1983	Tatra K2	
901–1027	M4	1982–87	Tatra T3	
1028–1047	M4	1993–97	Tatra T3	
1101–1130	M4	1994–96	Tatra T6	
1131–1138	M4	1998	Tatra T6	
1201–1214	AM4	1998–2001	Skoda Astra	Low floor
1251–1253	AM4	2002–3	Ostrava Trio	Low floor
1500	AM8	1984	Tatra KT8	
1501–1515	AM8	1989	Tatra KT8	

The Vitkovice iron and steel works are served by the Ostrava tramway.

PRAHA (PRAGUE)   1875   1435mm   136.6 km

The Czech capital is a beautiful city on the river Vltava, with a well-preserved central area, and extensive suburbs for housing and industry, with much new development. Investment in the large tramway system was overshadowed by metro construction for many years, but new extensions continue to be built to light rail standards. The latest, to Barrandov in the north, will open late in 2003. The central network has thinned as the metro expanded, but extensive sections of street track remain here and in the older suburbs. There are six bridges across the river that carry trams. The historic castle district on the hill west of the city centre is served by trams, including a tree-lined reservation; other routes to the north and west include some steep gradient sections. At one time the fleet comprised over 1000 standard Tatra T3 trams, but articulated cars were then purchased, followed by T6 trams, and the oldest trams withdrawn as passenger traffic fell due to increased car ownership following the change to the market economy. The city has almost recovered from severe flooding in August 2002, which put part of the tramway and most of the metro out of action for some months. A splendid tramway museum has been established in the Stresovice depot, and is open at weekends during the summer. Museum trams operate a city tour service during the summer months.

Rolling stock

5500	M4	1969	Tatra T4	Built for Beograd
5601–5602	M4	1989	Tatra T3	Private hire cars
6163, 6457, 6736	M4	1976	Tatra T3	
6289	M4	1970	Tatra T3	
6608–6715	M4	1967–68	Tatra T3	
6716–6922	M4	1970–74	Tatra T3	
6923–6992	M4	1976	Tatra T3	
7001–7252	M4	1982–87	Tatra T3	
7253–7292	M4	1989–90	Tatra T3	
8005–8106	M4	1976–81	Tatra	Renumbered from earlier cars
8200–01	M4	1994	Tatra	Renumbered from earlier cars
8300 series	M4	1971–76	Tatra	Renumbered from earlier cars
8210, 8511–30	M4	2000	Tatra	Rebodied by PARS Sumperk
8205, 8600	M4	1998	Tatra	T6
8601–8750	M4	1995–97	Tatra	T6
9001–9004	AM8	1986	Tatra	KT8
9005–9048	AM8	1989–90	Tatra	KT8
9101–9104	AM6	1997	Tatra	Low-floor prototypes; withdrawn

Opposite above **A T6 tram in the Czech capital of Prague.**

Opposite below **The Tatra design of low-floor tram (RT6) operated briefly in the Czech capital, but has now been withdrawn.**

Prague has the world's largest fleet of T3 trams, and they are still being rebuilt for further service.

Opposite **Narrow streets in the historic centre of Plzen require a one-way tramway layout.**

PLZEN   1899   1435mm   26 km

This industrial centre in western Bohemia is famous for brewing beer, and the Skoda industrial complex. The city centre is quite well preserved and surrounded by large modern residential districts. The tramway system went through a period of expansion a few years ago, from a street tramway serving the central area to reserved track lines in the new housing areas. The standard fleet of Tatra T3 trams has been supplemented by articulated cars, and more recently new low-floor trams.

Rolling stock

101–106	M4	1964	Tatra T3	Ex-Praha
107–110	M4	1964	Tatra T3	Ex-Most
160–171	M4	1964–67	Tatra T3	
172–207	M4	1970–76	Tatra T3	
208–245	M4	1982–83	Tatra T3	
246–287	M4	1985–87	Tatra KT8	
300–310	AM4	1997–2001	Skoda Astra	Low floor

Tatra KT4 trams line up at the Kopli terminus in Tallinn.

ESTONIA

This Baltic state was always regarded as the most relaxed part of the Soviet Union, with close ties with Finland across the gulf. Now independent again, it is developing economically, a process likely to be hastened by EU membership.

TALLINN   1888   1067mm   20 km

The capital of Estonia is renowned for its preserved, walled, city centre and charming atmosphere. The five-route tramway links the central area (outside the walls) with suburban estates, mostly on street track, but with the long former steam/petrol tramway to Kopli in the north-west including reserved track. Expansion plans have been held up by economic difficulties. The Tatra tram fleet is in need of modernisation, but so far just two low-floor centre sections, and some second-hand cars have arrived.

Rolling stock

52–123	AM4	1981–90	Tatra KT4	107/23, low-floor centre sections
124–132	AM4	1983–88	Tatra KT4	Ex-Gera
250–309	M4	1973–79	Tatra T4	

High in the hills above Tbilisi, this KTM-5 shows that there is some traffic potential in this rather remote suburb.

GEORGIA

The Georgian Republic, where local 'boy' Stalin is still revered, has had its share of unstable governments since the break-up of the Soviet Union, and tourist travel is still something of an adventure, although the capital, Tbilisi, is relatively safe. Tramway development has a very low priority in the current economic situation.

TBILISI   1883   1524mm   30 km

The Georgian capital lies in a bowl formed by surrounding hills. A metre-gauge tramway was replaced by Russian standard-gauge in the 1930s. In addition to serving street track in the valley, the trams climb steep gradients to reach hill-top suburbs, often on private right-of-way. The large system has been much reduced by metro construction in 1966–93, and split into two parts with the southern route acting purely as a metro feeder and maintained in reasonable condition (trams used here have pantographs). The more traditional main system, which includes hilly routes, is in a poor state (the trams have bow collectors) and, with little prospect of any new trams arriving, must have an uncertain future in this isolated city.

Rolling stock
113–190	M4	UKVZ KTM-5	1986–91	
581–599	M4	Riga RVZ-6	1987	Few remain

HUNGARY

The standard for Hungarian tramways was always set by the large Budapest system, with provincial systems often surviving on hand-me-downs from the capital. More recently tramway development in Budapest has been overshadowed by metro investment, and the provincial cities have developed their own styles. The giant Ganz-Mavag industrial combine, which built many Hungarian trams, was broken up for privatisation, and tramway work is now limited to electric equipment. Recent deliveries have been second-hand stock from western Europe, but new low-floor cars are on order for Budapest.

BUDAPEST   1866   1435mm   213 km

The Hungarian capital is a large city on the river Danube; on the west bank is the older and hilly Buda; on the east bank the larger and newer Pest. Many attractive buildings survive from the days of the Austro-Hungarian empire, with old and rather dull residential and industrial suburbs surrounding the central area, and new housing areas further out. The extensive tramway system went through a period of retrenchment as the Russian-style metro system was built and expanded, and local politics have affected decision-making. However a new ring tramway in Pest has been slowly built to light rail standards. The very heavy loadings which required intensive services with three-car sets have reduced with increasing car ownership following the fall of communism, but traffic is still heavy on the inner boulevard services. Tatra trams were acquired to complete the replacement of older rolling stock, and more recently the undertaking took advantage of second-hand light rail cars from Hannover to upgrade services. 40-year old Ganz sets will now be replaced by new low-floor cars. In addition to the modern metro, the shallow subway (Foldälatti) of 1896 is still in operation, with tramway-based rolling stock. In the north-west suburb of Buda a rack light railway carries passengers to hill-top leisure areas. Suburban electric light railways run north, east and south from termini on the edge of the central area, but no longer share any trackage with the urban tramway system. At Szentendre, the terminus of the northern suburban line, there is a tramway and light railway museum.

Rolling stock

1301–1370	AM8	1967–71	Ganz	
1401–1481	AM8	1972–78	Ganz	
1500–1575	AM8	1974–78	Duewag	Ex-Hannover
3200–3474	M4	1956–61	Ganz	
3750	AM6	1990	Ganz	
3800–3899	M4	1962–65	Ganz	
4000–4171	M4	1979–80	Tatra T5	
4200–4349	M4	1984	Tatra T5	
5806–5899	B2	1939–53	Ganz	
5900–5991	B2	1951–52	Ganz	
6000–6049	B2	1954	Ganz	
(40)	AM12	2004–6	Siemens	Low-floor cars on order

The coupled Ganz sets on Budapest routes 4 and 6 are due to be replaced by low-floor trams.

Fast disappearing from the scene are trams from the 1950s. The UV type in Budapest is the largest surviving fleet.

DEBRECEN   1911   1435mm   6 km

This provincial city in eastern Hungary has an historical city centre with green suburbs. The one-route tramway system links the railway station with the northern suburbs, providing an intensive service. A standard fleet of two-room-and-a-bath four-axle articulated trams has been partly replaced by a newly-developed Hungarian design of medium-floor articulated tram, but it seems as if no further orders for this design are likely.

Rolling stock

381–386	AM4	1967–69	Ganz
481–492	AM4	1969–79	Ganz
500	AM6	1993	Ganz-Hunslet
501–510	AM6	1997	Ganz-Hunslet

The last Ganz-built trams work the main tram route in Debrecen.

MISKOLC   1897   1435mm   9 km

Miskolc in north-east Hungary is an industrial city that has developed along a valley. This is served by a tram route running from the railway station and old city centre at the eastern end. A single-track loop serves an older housing area off the main line. A standard fleet of four-axle articulated trams has been mostly replaced by second-hand Tatra articulated cars, and the remainder by buying older articulated trams from Vienna. Ex-Vienna trailers are entering service.

Rolling stock

151/56/58	AM4	1970	Ganz	
169–174	AM4	1976–78	Ganz	
180–187	AM6	1969	SGP	Ex-Wien; more expected
200–209	AM8	1988	Tatra KT8	Ex-Kosice
210–217	AM8	1986–89	Tatra KT8	Ex-Most

Miskolc has modernised its tram fleet with Tatra KT8 cars and second-hand stock from Vienna.

SZEGED   1884   1435mm   14 km

Hungary's second city is in the south-east, on the river Tisza, near the Serbian/Romanian border. The well-preserved central area is surrounded by green suburbs and new housing areas. The tram system declined as trolleybuses were introduced, but now seems stable. In addition to a street-based line linking railway station and the city, there are other routes partly on reserved track, with some single-track sections. The standard four-axle articulated trams survive alongside a small fleet of Tatras.

Rolling stock

658–662	AM4	1970	Budapest/Debrecen	
801–815	AM4	1972	Budapest	
817, 820	AM4	1963/64	Budapest	Ex-Budapest
900–912	M4	1997	Tatra T6	

A Szeged T6 tram on a workshop test run is followed by a four-axle articulated car in use for driver training.

LATVIA

The Baltic state of Latvia is developing its own identity again after years of Soviet domination, and is hoping that membership of the EU will improve its economic situation, which has precluded significant tramway development since 1990.

DAUGAVPILS   1946   1524mm   12.5 km

This town on the banks of the river Daugav is an important railway junction, and the three-route tramway links the railway station with the eastern residential suburbs. The main route is double track, but other sections are single track with passing loops. A new depot was built in 1990. A start has been made on replacing the Riga RVZ-6 trams with second-hand Tatras from Germany. Trolley poles remain in use.

Rolling stock

009–065	M4	1977–87	Riga RVZ-6	40 remain
070–081	M4	1973–83	Tatra T3	Ex-Schwerin
101–112	M4	1990–92	UKVZ KTM-5	
114	M4	1994	UKVZ KTM-8	

A Coupled pair of RVZ-6 trams show that Daugavpils still uses trolley poles.

LIEPAYA   1899   1000mm   6.9 km

This historic port city (Libava until 1917) lies on an isthmus between lake and estuary, which are linked by a canal crossed by the tramway. The one route runs north–south past the railway station and through the well-preserved central area. A standard fleet of short articulated Tatras is operated, recently boosted by second-hand examples from Germany.

Rolling stock

220–235	AM4	1984–86	Tatra KT4	
236–238	AM4	1979–81	Tatra KT4	Ex-Cottbus
239	AM4	1983	Tatra KT4	Ex-Gera
240–243	AM4	1981–83	Tatra KT4	Ex-Erfurt

A refurbished Tatra KT4 tram passes traditional Latvian buildings in Liepaya.

Hanseatic architecture forms the backdrop to this pair of Riga Tatra T3M trams in advertising livery.

RIGA 1882 1524mm 61.5 km

The Latvian capital is an important port and industrial city, with an attractive city centre in Hanseatic style. The tramway system links this with suburban areas, including routes across the river Daugav to modern suburbs. The outer end of the line to the south features single track with loops on roadside reservation. No longer operating any locally-built RVZ trams, the standard fleet of Tatras has been extensively modernised mechanically and electrically in recent years. Trolley poles are still used.

Rolling stock

201–262	M4	1988–90	Tatra T3M	
2032–2192	M4	1976–87	Tatra T3	
2301–2349	M4	1982–86	Tatra T3	
2504–2508	M4	1987	Tatra T3	
2511/5/7	M4	1978–79	Tatra T3	Ex-Moskva

POLAND

The standardisation of Polish tramways under Communism is disappearing as the country succeeds in establishing a stable free-market economy in preparation for entry into the EU. However in many cities investment in public transport still struggles to make it to the top of the list, though there are encouraging signs from cities such as Poznan and Krakow. Delivery of trams from the only Polish manufacturer, Konstal, almost ceased in the 1990s, and even under new owners Alstom there is little sign that the full capacity of the Chorzow plant will ever be needed. Western-built low-floor trams are starting to appear.

BYDGOSZCZ   1880   1000mm   32 km

This seldom-visited industrial city has a well-preserved city centre with suburban industrial and housing areas. After a period of rapid expansion 30 years ago, the tramway has suffered from an investment hiatus because of the economic situation. The undertaking was planning conversion to standard gauge and upgrading to light rail standards, but now has to struggle with deferred track maintenance and no likelihood of any new rolling stock in the next few years. The tramway branch to the railway station has closed.

Rolling stock

223–361	M4	1977–83	Konstal	805N

CZESTOCHOWA   1959   1435mm   10.5 km

This is a modern industrial city, but is better known as a centre for Catholic pilgrimage based on the small old town area. The tramway system was built new in the late 1950s to link housing and industrial areas, with one route, mostly on reserved track. A fleet of standard Polish trams is run, featuring multiple-unit operation.

Rolling stock

601–616	M4	1989	Konstal	105N
636–697	M4	1976–85	Konstal	105N

ELBLAG   1895   1000mm   17.5 km

This small town suffered badly in the war, but the city centre has been completely reconstructed and the tramway system retained and expanded. There are four routes linking the city centre and railway stations with suburban housing areas, including some single-track sections. A new route to a shopping centre has been opened. The last two-axle trams were replaced a few years ago by second-hand articulated cars from Mainz in Germany.

Rolling stock

034–061	M4	1980–86	Konstal 805N	
221–225/7	AM6	1958–61	Westwaggon	Ex-Mainz
229/30/2–5	AM6	1965	Duewag	Ex-Mainz
237/8/41–5	AM6	1960–61	Duewag	Ex-Mainz, built for Heidelberg

A pair of standard Konstal 105N trams in the main street of Bydgoszcz.

The Czestochowa tramway is mostly segregated from other traffic.

This is one of the ex-Mainz Westwaggon-built trams in Elblag.

GDANSK 1873 1435mm 50 km

This industrial port city on the Baltic coast, famous for its shipyards, was once known as the Free City of Danzig, and suffered heavy damage during the war. More recently it was the cradle of the revolution that led to the downfall of Communism. The old city has been fully restored, but is not penetrated by the tramway system, which serves the railway station, port area and suburban housing areas, including much reserved track. The first new articulated trams have arrived to supplement the standard fleet of Polish bogie trams.

Rolling stock

1133/4/6/41	M4	1975–77	Konstal 105N	Ex-Krakow
1200–1428	M4	1976–86	Konstal 105N	208 cars
1001–1004	AM8	1999–2001	Alstom NGd99	Low-floor
1501–1502	AM8	1997	Alstom 114Na	Low-floor centre sections

Some of Konstal's early low-floor trams were delivered to Gdansk.

GORZOW   1899   1435mm   14 km

Gorzow is a small industrial town in western Poland with a tramway that was threatened with bus conversion 30 years ago. However it was decided to retain electric traction, and parts of the system have been upgraded from street to reserved track. The standard fleet of Polish-built trams has been partly replaced by second-hand articulated cars from Kassel in Germany.

Rolling stock

75–136	M4	1976–86	Konstal 105N	37 cars
221–224	AM6	1966–67	Credé	Ex-Kassel
251–257	AM6	1966–67	Wegmann	Ex-Kassel
261–266	AM6	1971	Wegmann	Ex-Kassel

This pair of Gorzow articulated trams were built for Kassel.

Grudziadz 73 ran on two German systems before arriving in Poland.

GRUDZIADZ   1899   1000mm   12 km

Poland's smallest tramway was for long a two-route system, a north–south line crossing the picturesque town centre, and a branch to the railway station, featuring much single track with passing loops. Now a new double-track line to serve housing development has been built. Many of the system's trams were destroyed in a depot fire in 1993, but tramway operation was retained, using rolling stock drafted in from other Polish undertakings, and the depot rebuilt in its original style. More recently a few second-hand articulated trams have arrived from Germany.

Rolling stock

37–60	M4	1976–86	Konstal 805N	Acquired from various systems
63–69	M4	1993	Konstal 805N	
71–72	AM6	1967	Duewag	Ex-Mannheim
73–78	AM6	1962–63	Duewag	Ex-Würzburg, built for Hagen

KATOWICE   1894   1435mm   245 km

Katowice is the largest town in the extensive industrial conurbation of Upper Silesia, and its transport undertaking provides a network of services throughout the area, serving Zabrze, Gliwice, Bytom, Chorzow, Sosnowiec and Dabrowa. The tramway system is an important part of the network and has a range of services, from dense urban operations to long interurban lines operating through semi-rural/industrial landscapes. There is a plan to create a regional semi-metro by upgrading tramways to light rail standards, but the economic situation has meant slow progress, with only Katowice–Chorzow dealt with so far (including new low-floor trams). In the meantime some outer sections have succumbed to bus replacement. The fleet has often been the proving ground for prototype trams from manufacturer Konstal of Chorzow, but today, apart from the latest delivery, is very standardised. Exceptions are Poland's last two-axle trams, which shuttle along a short route in Bytom which cannot be rebuilt with turning circles for the otherwise single-ended fleet.

Rolling stock

112–247	AM6	1969–73	Konstal 102N	33 cars
313–792	M4	1975–85	Konstal 105N	334 cars (6 are double-ended 111N)
800–816	AM6	2001–02	Alstom 116Nd	
954, 1118	M2	1954	Konstal N	

One of the surviving two-axle KSW trams in Katowice. *(Karel Hoorn)*

Krakow is buying low-floor articulated trams from Bombardier.

KRAKOW   1882   1435mm   83 km

This ancient and beautiful city on the river Vistula became an important industrial centre with the establishment of the nearby Nowa Huta steelworks and associated new town. Today Nowa Huta has fallen on hard times, but still has its own internal tram routes, while other lines provide the link to the traditional city centre of Krakow, with its own suburbs. The street track here and in older suburbs is supplemented by reserved track on the interurban links and within the old town. A fleet of articulated cars equipped for multiple-unit operation moved heavy traffic on busy routes, supplemented by more modern bogie cars, but have largely been replaced as traffic has fallen. Nürnberg in Germany has been a source of second-hand trams, while the first low-floor cars have been bought to work a new route to Kurdwanow, which is being extended (with more cars on order).

Rolling stock

156–199	JM6	1962–65	MAN	Ex-Nürnberg
301–342	AM6	1962–64	MAN	Ex-Nürnberg
351–499	M4	1975–80	Konstal 105N	
601–39/74–				
93, 726–947	M4	1981–85	Konstal 105N	
2001–2014	JM6	2001	Bombardier	Low-floor
2015–2026	JM6	2003	Bombardier	Low floor

LODZ 1898 1000mm 149 km

This traditional industrial city has a dense urban tram network though most of the interesting track layouts resulting from the narrow streets in the central area have been designed out in recent years. Large outer suburbs are often served by reserved-track tramways and there are some long interurban routes extending south and west into the semi-rural hinterland on roadside reservation or private right-of-way. These have been hived off to a separate operating company, which started by using the ex-Bielefeld articulated trams, but is rebuilding Polish trams of this type. The rest of the fleet comprises standard Polish-built trams, and just arriving are the first low-floor Cityrunner cars.

Rolling stock

1–41	AM6	1974	Konstal 803N	Interurban company
43, 44, 47	AM6	1957–60	Düwag	ex-Bielefeld
220–460	M4	1972–80	Konstal 805N	
501–583	M4	1975–76	Konstal 805N	36 cars
700–743	M4	1981–82	Konstal 805N	
800–839	M4	1983–84	Konstal 805N	
900–939	M4	1985–86	Konstal 805N	
1001–1014	M4	1988–89	Konstal 805N	
3015–3030	M4	1991–92	Konstal 805N	
1201–1215	AM6	2001–02	Bombardier	Low floor

Western-designed low-floor trams are starting to appear on East European systems. This Bombardier Cityrunner is in the Polish city of Lodz. (Rudolf Rappelt)

A coupled pair of refurbished 105N trams on the city system in Lodz.

POZNAN   1880   1435mm   90 km

This modern industrial city on the river Warta, with its large residential suburbs, has one of the most progressive tram undertakings in Poland, and has long wished to upgrade to light rail standards. Some suburban lines have been improved and more recently a wholly-new route was built, incorporating a short subway. The fleet of standard Polish trams was supplemented by some ex-Amsterdam articulated cars, and then Duewag trams from Düsseldorf and Frankfurt-am-Main (with more arriving). Now the first batch of low-floor trams are on order from Siemens, which has also been awarded a long-term maintenance contract.

Rolling stock

1–71	AM6	1970–73	Konstal 102N 6 cars	
81–341	M4	1975–90	Konstal 105N	
400	AM8	1995	Konstal/Cegielski	
401–410	AM6	1997–98	Tatra/Cegielski	Low-floor, withdrawn
501–514	AM6	2003–4	Siemens	Low-floor, on order
601–617	AM6	1959–63	Duewag	Ex-Frankfurt
650–682/92	AM8	1957–59	Duewag	Ex-Düsseldorf/Frankfurt
851–881	AM6	1957–62	Schindler	Ex-Amsterdam, more expected
1811–1826	B4	1960–66	Duewag	Ex-Frankfurt

Poznan 400 is an eight-axle prototype based on the 105N design.

SZCZECIN   1879   1435mm   40 km

This important industrial city, with its shipyards on the river Odra, still shows much evidence of its Hanseatic past, when it was known as Stettin, although post-war reconstruction has given it a modern aspect. The tramway system expanded after the war to serve new housing areas, but development has slowed due to the economic situation. The system is mostly in the street, with some reservation on newer lines, including the cross-river route, which may be extended as a light rail line. The tram fleet was modernised with standard Polish cars, with the last two-axle cars replaced by cars from other Polish fleets. Now second-hand stock from Düsseldorf has arrived, plus a batch of new Polish trams.

Rolling stock

503–515	AM8	1957–60	Duewag	Ex-Düsseldorf
590–600	M4	1976–85	Konstal 105N	
601–630	AM6	1971–73	Konstal 102N	Some ex-other systems
631–780	M4	1975–92	Konstal 105N	Some ex-other systems
783–790	M4	2001	Konstal 105N	
901–919	AM6	1958–61	Duewag	Ex-Düsseldorf
1001–1052	M4	1994–95	Konstal 105N	
1053–1058	M4	2001	Konstal 105N	

Konstal's latest design has reverted to high-floor bogie trams as shown in Szczecin.

TORUN   1891   1000mm   11 km

This small industrial town on the river Vistula has retained and modernised its tramways, with reserved-track extensions to industrial sites, and new tracks avoiding narrow streets in the city centre. However the line to the railway station south of the river was closed and current economic conditions have brought investment to a halt. Articulated trams have been withdrawn, leaving a standardised fleet of Polish bogie cars.

Rolling stock

212–271	M4	1980–89	Konstal 805Na	

WARSZAWA   1865   1435mm   122 km

The Polish capital on the river Vistula suffered severely in the Second World War, but the historic old town has been beautifully restored. It is surrounded by a modern city centre and extensive suburbs, including both industrial areas and tower block housing estates. A Russian-style metro was under construction for many years, finally opening in 1995, and its extension is still taking up much public transport investment funding. Although the large tramway system is the backbone of public transport, only small-scale expansion has been possible. Much of the system is on reserved track, including the wide thoroughfares of the central area; street track is found in older suburbs. A large fleet of standard Polish bogie trams was built up, equipped for multiple unit operation, but when Alstom took over Konstal, the new design of low-floor car was acquired. This did not find favour and more bogie cars were purchased while funding was put together for an order for western-style low-floor trams. During the summer a city tram tour is operated with historic cars.

Rolling stock

140–843	M4	1966–69	Konstal 13N	About 500 cars
1000–1470	M4	1974–94	Konstal 105N	
2001–2009	M4	1990	Konstal 105N	
2010–2073	M4	1992–93	Konstal 105N	
2074–2135	M4	2001–02	Konstal 105N	
3001	AM6	1995	Konstal 112N	Low-floor section
3002–3004	AM6	1997	Alstom 116Na	Low-floor
3005–3030	AM6	1998–2000	Alstom 116Na	Low-floor

WROCLAW   1877   1435mm   85 km

This historic city on the river Odra, with its well-preserved central area, was the German city of Breslau until the end of the Second World War, and much of the prominent architecture dates from that era. The large tramway system serves all the areas of the city and has been extended into new housing estates. The system is mostly street track, with some reservation in suburban areas. There is a cross-country line to Lesnica in the eastern hinterland. The tram fleet comprises standard Polish types.

Rolling stock

2001–2110	AM6	1970–73	Konstal 102Na	59 cars
2201–2507	M4	1976–90	Konstal 105N	
2508–2561	M4	1977–80	Konstal 105N	Some ex-other systems

Torun has this replica historical tram. A 105N passes in the background.

Konstal copied the Tatra T1 to produce the 13N design, which still operates in Warsaw.

Wroclaw has used a large fleet of high-capacity bogie trams.

ROMANIA

Seven new tramways in seven years (1984–91) were a manifestation of the electric city transport policy of the previous regime in Romania, but since the revolution economic circumstances have made survival the hardest task for transport undertakings. With the collapse of Romanian industry, and the poor quality of stock built since the 1970s, a huge influx of some 1000 trams from German systems (often retaining original liveries and fleet numbers) has changed the face of the tramway systems, providing at least a short-term solution to problems.

ARAD 1896 1000mm 45.5 km

This attractive city near the Hungarian border has expanded considerably with the growth of industrial suburbs and housing areas. The tramway system kept pace with this expansion, with many new lines, including a long interurban running east to villages in the hinterland that were once served by an electric light railway. Although there are nominally some 15 routes, frequencies on some are poor and reliability problems became evident as rolling stock fell into bad condition. However the arrival of German trams from a variety of systems has improved availability and added a catalogue of different liveries, as most were put into service without repainting.

Rolling stock

1–31	M4	1984–86	Timis	Most withdrawn
2–32	B4	1984–86	Timis	Most withdrawn
33–53	AM6	1967–69	Duewag	8, ex-Bochum-Gelsenkirchen
37, 41, 42	M2	1957–61	Gotha	Ex-Halberstadt
80–179	M4	1974–81	Tatra T4	
107–138	AM6	1960–63	Duewag	10, ex-Ludwigshafen
149/63	B4	1977–79	Tatra T4	Ex-Halle
230	M4	1955	Duewag	Ex-Mülheim/Ruhr
258–264	AM6	1958–64	Duewag	5, ex-Mülheim/Ruhr
240	JM6	1960	Duewag	Ex-Mainz
271–276	AM6	1962–63	Duewag	3, ex-Würzburg (ex-Hagen)
301–304	AM6	1962	Duewag	Ex-OEG Mannheim
311–314	B4	1962	Duewag	Ex-OEG Mannheim
406–697	AM4	1960–63	Esslingen	31, ex-Stuttgart
918–926	M2	1967–68	Tatra	8, ex-Zwickau
921/58	M2	1965/60	Gotha	Ex-Zwickau
962–991	B2	1964–69	Gotha	7, ex-Zwickau
994/7	B2	1968	Tatra	Ex-Zwickau
1014	AM6	1963	Duewag	Ex-RHB Ludwigshafen
1054	AB6	1963	Duewag	Ex-RHB Ludwigshafen
1027/93	M4	1976–79	Tatra T4	Ex-Halle
1751–1865	JM8	1962–66	Duewag	17, ex-Essen
1859–1863	JM8	1960–66	Duewag	7, ex-Essen

The unusual Düwag motor+trailer articulated car sets built for the Rhein-Haardt-Bahn have found their way to Arad.

Arad route 6 has all the atmosphere of a Hungarian gutter-running tramway (which it once was). The Tatra T4 is one of the original deliveries to Romania.

This ex-Magdeburg Tatra T4 was still carrying its German fleet number when photographed in Botosani.

BOTOSANI   1991   1435mm   11 km

Romania's newest tramway is in this small town near the Ukrainian border, where construction started before the fall of communism in conjunction with large-scale urban renewal. Two routes link an industrial area with the railway station and town centre on street track, but build quality is low. The original Romanian-built fleet soon fell apart, and the system had a period of closure, but now runs mostly with Tatras acquired from Germany.

Rolling stock

1–16	AM8	1987–90	Bucuresti	Most withdrawn
17–22	M4	1969–77	Tatra T4	Ex-Magdeburg
23–36	M4	1972–78	Tatra T4	Ex-Dresden
37–47	M4	1977–81	Tatra T4	Ex-Dresden

BRAILA 1900 1435mm 15 km

The small urban tramway in this industrial town on the Danube delta was expanded by building extensions to suburban industrial sites, and a second route through the central area. The system is mostly street track, with private right-of-way across country to the southern terminus at the paper factory. A mixed fleet of Czech and Romanian-built trams has been largely replaced by second-hand stock acquired from German systems.

Rolling stock

19–28	M4	1978	Tatra	4 remain
29–81	M4	1979–89	Timis	11 remain
36–88	B4	1979–89	Timis	10 remain
82–91	AM6	1989	Bucuresti	Ex-AM8
235–268	M4	1958–60	MAN	10, ex-Nürnberg
1564–1579	B4	1961–63	MAN	6, ex-Nürnberg
1591–1610	B4	1964–66	MAN	10, ex-Nürnberg
9050–9160	AM4	1978–88	Tatra KT4	20, ex-Berlin

Braila operates a fleet of bogie trams donated by Nürnberg.

BRASOV   1987   1435mm   6.7 km

The single tram route in this established industrial town links a factory with the railway station and the edge of the town centre, but is duplicated by a trolleybus line that penetrates the central area and captures most of the traffic. The original fleet of Romanian articulated trams has been replaced by second-hand German trams.

Rolling stock

1–12	B4	1979–86	Tatra B4	6, ex-Leipzig
43–54	M4	1977–78	Tatra T4	12, ex-Leipzig
33–42	JM6	1960–63	Duewag	Ex-Frankfurt

BUCURESTI (BUCHAREST) 1874   1435mm   160 km

The Romanian capital is a large city whose formerly elegant city centre was much defaced by the grandiose reconstruction projects of the previous regime, although many fine buildings remain. The central area is surrounded by sprawling suburbs and industrial areas, with much new housing built in recent years. The large tramway system started to decline in importance as a metro system was built, and was banished from much of the city centre in favour of trolleybuses. However the largely street track system has been supplemented by new suburban extensions, many on reserved track, and limited development continues. RATB rebodied older bogie trams, imported a large fleet of new Tatras and produced its own articulated cars before the change in economic circumstances forced it to rely on second-hand stock from Germany. More recently World Bank funding for modernisation has seen substantial rebuilding of the articulated tram fleet.

Rolling stock

001–362	AM8	1973–88	Bucuresti	Many modernised
1203–1226	B4	1956–57	Duewag	10, ex-Frankfurt
2008/33	AM4	1966–68	Rathgeber	Ex-München
2413–2497	M4*	1956–59	Rathgeber	22, ex-München
2510–2670	M4*	1963–65	Rathgeber	27, ex-München
3001/2	AM6	1971(99)	Tatra	Rebuilt from M4
3006/7	AB4	1966	Rathgeber	Ex-München
3301–3431	M4	1971–74	Tatra T4	
3409–3497	B4*	1956–59	Rathgeber	31, ex-München
3503–3544	B4*	1963–64	Rathgeber	22, ex-München
4001–4049	AM6	1985–86	Bucuresti	

* Purchased as M3/B3 but now refitted with bogies from withdrawn trams

Opposite above **The standard Romanian-built eight-axle tram depicted in Brasov.**

Opposite below **The Bucharest workshops built large numbers of eight-axle trams, which are now being modernised.** *(M. Vleugels)*

This Tatra KT4 in Cluj displays both Berlin and local fleet numbers.

CLUJ-NAPOCA 1987   1435mm   11.5 km

The twin towns on the Somesul river are a regional centre for local industry, and many buildings in the central area date from the days of the Austro-Hungarian empire. The single tram line links the centre with the railway station and industrial and residential suburbs, all on street track. Service became very irregular as the original fleet could not be maintained in serviceable condition, but the arrival of second-hand stock from Berlin and Magdeburg has restored a semblance of normality.

Rolling stock

01–41	M4	1987	Timis	Most withdrawn
02–42	B4	1987	Timis	Most withdrawn
3–52	AM4	1977–78	Tatra KT4	26, ex-Berlin
61–76	M4	1968–75	Tatra T4	18, ex-Magdeburg
68–69	B4	1974–78	Tatra T4	Ex-Magdeburg

Ex-Berlin KT4 trams are replacing Romanian-built stock in Constanta.

CONSTANTA   1984   1435mm   42 km

This town borders the Black Sea resort of Mamaia, but is a commercial port and industrial centre. The three-route tramway system was the first of a new wave of Romanian tramways built in the 1980s and provides links between the railway station, central area and industrial districts. A fourth route was added later. The undertaking succeeded in providing a reasonable service with its Romanian-built articulated cars, but these have now been supplemented by second-hand Tatras from Berlin.

Rolling stock

101–175	AM8	1984–89	Bucuresti	9 ex-Oradea
176–190	AM4	1977–78	Tatra KT4	Ex-Berlin

CRAIOVA   1987   1435mm   19 km

This industrial and university city in southern Romania built a north-west to south-east tram route across the central area and out to industrial suburbs, with street track in the centre and reservation further out. Industrial decline has led to reduced frequencies outside the central areas. Most of the original Romanian-built fleet has been replaced by second-hand German trams.

Rolling stock

001–49	M4	1987–89	Timis	Most withdrawn
001–049	B4	1987–88	Timis	Most withdrawn
101–110	AM4	1977–78	Tatra T4	Ex-Berlin
111–127	M4	1977–81	Tatra T4	Ex-Leipzig
111–127	B4	1976–82	Tatra T4	Ex-Leipzig

The Romanian built Timis bogie trams in use in Craiova.

Bogie trams from Frankfurt meet an ex-Berlin KT4 in Galati.

GALATI   1899   1435mm   35 km

This port and industrial city on the Danube delta had a metre-gauge tramway system from 1899 to 1978. In 1972 the first section of a new standard-gauge system was opened to link new housing areas with a large steelworks complex built in the western suburbs. The standard-gauge system expanded as the town grew and the metre-gauge operation was withdrawn. Although many different routes are operated, many are limited services associated with shift changes at the steel works, which has declined due to economic circumstances. Poor maintenance saw the line closed for a period prior to reconstruction. Some of the original Tatra fleet survive, supplemented by second-hand German trams.

Rolling stock

1–51	M4	1970–76	Tatra T4	7, ex-Magdeburg
3–50	M4	1972–73	Tatra T4	
5–92	AM4	1977–78	Tatra KT4	32, ex-Berlin
9–95	M4	1971–78	Tatra T4	12, ex-Dresden
84–88	M4	1956–57	Duewag	Ex-Frankfurt
324–328	B4	1957–64	Duewag	Ex-Frankfurt
396–399	B4	1971–78	Tatra B4	4, ex-Dresden

IASI   1900   1000mm   67 km

This city is a university town in north-east Romania by the Moldavian border. Its tramway system was expanded considerably from the original hilly system to reach new housing areas surrounding the old city centre. The system has changed its layout significantly as it expanded and there is a modern layout through much of the city. In addition to importing new Tatras, Iasi was the last undertaking to take delivery of new Romanian-built trams (to replace the last two-axle cars). However second-hand trams from a variety of German undertakings have since arrived.

Rolling stock

101–116	JM6	1961–63	DWM	Ex-Darmstadt
201–274	M4	1974–79	Tatra T4	27, ex-Halle
202–270	M4	1979–81	Tatra T4	
273/4	B4	1974–77	Tatra B4	Ex-Halle
301–333	AM4	1962–64	Esslingen	25, ex-Stuttgart
301–348	M4	1982–83	Timis	Most withdrawn
350	JM6	1985	Bucuresti	
351–353	JM6	1994	Bucuresti	
354–373	JM5	1956	Rathgeber	13, ex-Augsburg
851–890	AM4	1959–65	Esslingen	27, ex-Halle, built for Stuttgart

Iasi 103, still in its Darmstadt livery, is followed by a Tatra T4.

Oradea has second-hand Tatra trams from Berlin and Magdeburg.

ORADEA   1905   1435mm   20 km

This former Hungarian city in north-west Romania has an attractive city centre and new housing areas in western suburbs. The tramway system operates a trunk route linking two railway stations, and had railway and factory connections for tramway goods traffic, plus a ring service to the north. All this is mostly street track, but an extension to the west is on reservation. Although a reasonable service was maintained using Romanian-built cars, these have now been replaced by second-hand trams from German systems.

Rolling stock

1–49	M4	1969–82	Tatra T4	Ex-Magdeburg
(13)	M4	1970–79	Tatra T4	Ex-Magdeburg
101–125	B4	1969–76	Tatra B4	Ex-Magdeburg
126–132	B4	1974–86	Tatra B4	Ex-Magdeburg
200–231	AM4	1977–78	Tatra KT4	Ex-Berlin

Ploesti is another system with ex-German KT4 trams, this time from Potsdam.

PLOEISTI   1987   1435mm   18.5 km

This town north of Bucuresti is the base for the Romanian oil industry and built a three-route tramway linking both railway stations with the town centre and industrial suburbs. The attractive central area has street track in narrow streets. Romanian-built trams were well maintained here, but have been supplemented by second-hand stock from Germany.

Rolling stock

45070–45079	AM4	1977–83	Tatra KT4	Ex-Potsdam
45085–45098	AM4	1980–82	Tatra KT4	Ex-Potsdam
45099–45106	AM4	1977–85	Tatra KT4	Ex-Potsdam
55001–55020	M4	1987–88	Timis	Withdrawn 2003
55401–55419	B4	1987–88	Timis	Withdrawn 2003
55031–55059	AM8	1987–88	Bucuresti	Withdrawn 2003

RESITA   1988   1435mm   9.5 km

Resita is the centre of an industrial district producing most of Romania's steel and the tramway was built to link this with housing areas. The line runs along the river valley, crossing the river and adjacent railway three times. Although opened in 1988, the tramway struggled for four years due to the lack of a depot, and later had serious problems maintaining its Romanian-built trams, which led to a suspension of service. Today service is maintained by first-generation eight-axle trams acquired from Dortmund.

Rolling stock

10–30	AM8	1966–74	Duewag	Ex-Dortmund

SIBIU   1905   1000mm   10 km

This former German settlement in Transylvania has an historic and attractive city centre. A trolleybus service operates between the railway station and the central cemetery, which is the terminus of the single-track rural tramway to the village of Rasinari. The village terminus is a reversing triangle in the street, but most of the line is on roadside reservation. After a period of closure due to the poor state of the track, service resumed using the first second-hand trams to be imported into Romania, Swiss Standard cars from Geneva.

Rolling stock

302/6/7/15	B4	1950–51	FFA	Ex-Geneva	
712/21/4/7	M4	1950–52	SWP	Ex-Geneva	Withdrawn 2003

TIMISOARA   1899   1435mm   45 km

This attractive city is on the Banat river in western Romania, close to the Hungarian and Serbian borders; there are Hungarian and German-speaking minorities. Probably Romania's most progressive tramway, the layout of the system changed substantially as old sections with awkward layouts were replaced by new lines, often on reservation. A branch to the railway station links with urban circular routes and lines to suburban housing areas. The city was the home to the Timis tram-building factory, which supplied all its fleet, but when bankruptcy forced closure, a switch was made to importing trams from German undertakings, including modern four-axle articulated cars (both motors and trailers). A tramway museum (open Saturdays) is located at Take Ionescu depot.

Rolling stock

102/5–7	JM8	1958–59	Duewag	Ex-Karlsruhe
109–115	JM8	1959	Rastatt	5, ex-Karlsruhe
153–172	JM6	1959–64	DWM	9, ex-Karlsruhe
167, 174	JM8	1963–64	DWM	Ex-Karlsruhe
1–130	B4	1972–89	Timis	50 remain
231–359	M4	1972–79	Timis	50 remain
2003–2042	AM4	1966–68	Rathgeber	17, ex-München
3015–3040	AB4	1966–68	Rathgeber	16, ex-München
3420–3479	AM4	1963–68	Hansa	42, ex-Bremen
3502–3511	AM4	1973	Wegmann	5, ex-Bremen
3701–3708	AB4	1973	Wegmann	5, ex-Bremen
3601–3646	AB4	1959–68	Hansa	39, ex-Bremen

Left **The industrial landscape of Resita is not so different from parts of Dortmund, where these Düwag trams originated.**

Centre **The end of the line in Sibiu-Rasinari, with Swiss standard trams about to use the reversing triangle.**

Below **The unusual sets of four-axle articulated trams from Bremen have found a new home in Timisoara.**

RUSSIA

The Russian federation forms the largest part of the former Soviet Union and is the state with the largest number of tramway systems, of which some 40 may be regarded as being in European Russia (Asia starting beyond the Ural mountains). These include the world's largest tramway system, in St Petersburg. But the problems facing that system are symbolic of the difficulties faced by many Russian tramways. Farebox revenue generates only a small fraction of operating costs (many passengers are entitled to free travel through state concessions, but the undertakings receive no reimbursement for this), and the municipalities are on the verge of bankruptcy, so cannot pay the proper subsidies. As a result, investment has fallen to levels which are completely insufficient to maintain safe and efficient operation. Since 1990 four Russian tramways have closed (Karpinsk, Grozniy, Karahganda and Shakhty), but unless a solution is found to the economic problems many more could follow in the next decade. Politicians are largely indifferent, seeing privatised (and competing) buses as the way forward. Local management is probably poorly trained to find innovative ways of coping with such problems. The future looks bleak unless economic prosperity is achieved throughout Russian society.

ARKHANGEL'SK   1916   1524mm   12 km

The world's most northerly tramway system, 50 km from the White Sea, has suffered severe cutbacks in 2002–03, with the closure of the single-track lines on Solombala island to the north (until 1956 a separate network), and part of the main line alongside the Severnaya Dvina river. Harsh climatic conditions and indifferent maintenance mean that the remaining section of tramway is unlikely to survive many more months, as the trolleybus system (opened 1974) expands. Most surviving trams were built in St Petersburg.

Rolling stock

362–410	M4	1984–87	Riga RVZ-6	Few remain
500–505	AM6	1993	PTMZ LVS-86	
506–525	M4	1995	PTMZ LM-93	

Arkhangel'sk bought its most modern trams from the PMTZ factory in St Petersburg.

The KTM-8 trams of the early 1990s are Astrakhan's most modern cars. *(A. Olander)*

ASTRAKHAN   1900   1524mm   31 km

This ancient port city on the Volga delta near the Caspian Sea has a city centre circle route A and four other routes which run out to suburban housing areas. The original Belgian-built metre-gauge system was regauged to Russian standard in 1952–59. The system features the usual mix of street track in the central area and semi-reservation in the suburbs. The tram fleet is in good condition, with some modernisation taking place. Trolleybuses have been operated since 1967.

Rolling stock
065–147	M4	1985–92	UKVZ KTM-5
1018–23/7/8/32/3	M4	1991–92	UKVZ KTM-5
1024–6/9/31/4–43	M4	1993–94	UKVZ KTM-8
1100	M4	1993	UKVZ KTM-8

Well-maintained KTM-5 trams in Cherepovets.

CHEREPOVETS   1956   1524mm   12.7 km

An industrial town in Russia's northern region, Cherepovets gained its tramway thanks to the local steel works, which financed its construction and still owns and operates the line today. Essentially a reserved-track east–west line, there is a single track one-way street loop in the centre to serve the railway station. Rolling stock and infrastructure are well maintained and a good level of service is provided.

Rolling stock
69–147	M4	1984–92	UKVZ KTM-5
148–153	M4	1992–93	UKVZ KTM-8

DZERZHINSK   1933   1524mm   39 km

The tramway system in this Volga region town on the river Oka comprises a quite dense network in the central area and a long route east to more scattered communities, with a short-working service. There are two tram depots, one built as recently as 1989, but rolling stock replacement is now needed. Trolleybuses have been operated since 1976.

Rolling stock
001–087	M4	1987–92	UKVZ KTM-5
088/93/4	M4	1992–93	UKVZ KTM-8
089/90–2	M4	1992–93	UKVZ KTM-8
223–300	M4	1981–87	UKVZ KTM-5

Many Russian systems, including Dzerzhinsk, still use bow collectors on their KTM-5 trams.

Ivanovo KTM-5 286 turns out of Prospekt Lenina on the city circle. *(A. Olander)*

IVANOVO   1934   1524mm   19.4 km

This is an administrative and industrial town in central Russia, 240 km north-east of Moscow, with a central area loop tramway fed by four short suburban routes, which all terminate at the railway station. No new trams have been purchased for 10 years, but the fleet is kept in reasonable condition. Trolleybuses were introduced in 1962.

Rolling stock

253–314	M4	1984–92	UKVZ KTM-5
315–323	M4	1993	UKVZ KTM-8

IZHEVSK   1935   1524mm   33 km

On the western edge of the Ural mountains, this industrial city is the capital of the Udmurt Republic, and is known for its steel products. The tramway system was enhanced in 1982 by an 8-km light rail line north-east to Voroshilova. An intensive multi-route service is provided by a tram fleet that has undergone a degree of modernisation, including purchase of second-hand trams, some of which have been rebodied. Trolleybuses were introduced in 1968.

Rolling stock

1000–1003	M4	1997	Tatra T3R	
1104–1207	M4	1971–85	Tatra T3	1203–7 ex-Moskva
2001–2035	M4	1987–93	Tatra T3M	
2081	M4	1967	Tatra T3	
2100	M4	2000	UKVZ KTM-19	
2201–2210	M4	1980–85	Tatra T3	Ex-Moskva
2213–2350	M4	1968–84	Tatra T3	
2351–2353	M4	2000–01	Tatra T3R	Parts ex Czech Republic
(10)	M4	2003–4	Tatra T3M	on order

Shabby Tatra T3 trams in Ulitsa Karl Marksa in Izhevsk. *(A. Olander)*

KALININGRAD   1881   1000mm   52 km

The former German city of Königsberg, capital of East Prussia, was renamed and resettled in 1946, and today is the capital of a Russian enclave, just 30 km from the Polish border, and otherwise surrounded by Lithuanian territory. The city's economy has suffered through its isolation from the motherland and the tramway through its metre gauge, shared with only one other Russian system. However the system has been maintained almost intact, and modernisation has taken place by the import of second-hand trams from Germany. Trolleybus operation dates from 1975.

Rolling stock

144–323	M4	1972–79	Tatra T4	65 remain
401–441	AM4	1987–94	Tatra KT4	
442–443	AM6	1963	Düwag	Ex-Mannheim
501–530	M4	1974–79	Tatra T4	Ex-Halle
601–612	AM4	1979–83	Tatra KT4	Ex-Cottbus

A Tatra KT4 tram in front of Korolevskiye Vorota in Kaliningrad. *(B. Kussmagk)*

Kazan RVZ-6 tram on street track in the city centre. *(A. Olander)*

KAZAN   1875   1524mm   73.8 km

This is an historic city at the confluence of the Volga and Kazanka rivers, with three tramway bridges across the latter. The capital of the Tatar republic, outside the old central area it is heavily industrialised and relies on its tramway to carry workers to and from residential areas, including a recently-built long ring route to the north and east. A metro is planned, but little progress has been made with this since the collapse of the Soviet Union. Trams are maintained in good condition and fleet modernisation has continued, leading to the most varied tram fleet in Russia. Trolleybuses were introduced in 1948.

Rolling stock (cars in range 001–404 carry depot prefix numbers)

001–024	M4	1993	UKVZ KTM-8
025–026	M4	1995	UKVZ KTM-8M
049–076	M4	1996–2002	UKVZ KTM-8M
150–179	M4	1983–87	Riga RVZ-6
201–210	M4	2002	UTM Spektr
301–307	M4	1993–97	PTMZ LM-93
308–322	M4	2000–02	PTMZ LM-99
348–363	M4	1996–2001	UKVZ KTM-8M
401–404	M4	1999–2000	UKVZ KTM-19
1167–1219	M4	1987–92	UKVZ KTM-5
2001–2048	M4	1988–92	UKVZ KTM-5
3301–3347	M4	1987–92	UKVZ KTM-5

KOLOMNA   1948   1524mm   18.3 km

Kolomna is a small town on the Moskva river south-east of the capital, to which it is linked by commuter rail service. The tramway system features a town ring with short branches to local industry and the railway station. The tram fleet has benefited from continuing modernisation, and a new extension was opened in 2002.

Rolling stock

2–98	M4	1978–87	Riga RVZ-6	About 6 remain
100–133	M4	1987–91	UKVZ KTM-5	
134–135	M4	1993	UKVZ KTM-8	
136–137	M4	1991	UKVZ KTM-8	Ex-Moskva
138–152	M4	1995–99	UKVZ KTM-8M	
001–002	AM6	1998	PTMZ LVS-97	
003–016	M4	2001	PTMZ LM-99	

The unusual **PTMZ-built LVS-97** design of six-axle articulated tram has been tried by Kolomna. *(A. Olander)*

KRASNODAR   1900   1524mm   55.2 km

A city in the Caucasus, 80 km from the Black Sea, Krasnodar is the centre of an agricultural district, and an important railway junction. The Belgian metre-gauge tramway was regauged in the mid-1930s. The tramway has seen a new extension recently to take routes 20 and 21 across the railway to the northern suburbs. Fleet modernisation is becoming an issue. A trolleybus operation was opened in 1950.

Rolling stock

001–159	M4	1980–86	Tatra T3	107–134 ex-Grozniy
226–236	M4	1994	UKVZ KTM-8	
300–352	M4	1981–90	UKVZ KTM-5	335–52 secondhand
491, 495	M4	1990	UKVZ KTM-5	Ex-Rostov
500–599	M4	1979–87	UKVZ KTM-5	

This Krasnodar Tatra T3 started life in the Chechen capital of Grozniy. *(A. Olander)*

Two Tatra T3M trams pass in Chernozyom city of Kursk. (A. Olander)

KURSK   1898   1524mm   40.4 km

This city 450 km south of Moscow was largely destroyed in the Second World War, with just a small section of the old centre surviving. Before the break-up of the Soviet Union, the tramway was extended south on a long reserved route to an industrial area, which now has direct routes to residential districts. The undertaking is fortunate in having an all-Tatra fleet, which provides better quality than Russian-built trams. Trolleybuses started operating in 1972.

Rolling stock

009–084	M4	1987–95	Tatra T3M	
103–149	M4	1976–82	Tatra T3	
200–222	M4	1986–83	Tatra T3	
270–313	M4	1975–83	Tatra T3	
400–427	M4	1981–87	Tatra T3	413–27 ex-Moskva

LIPETSK   1947   1524mm   48.5 km

This modern city on the River Voronezh south-east of Moscow grew significantly in the 1930s and tramway construction started immediately after the war. A long loop line links the central area with western and southern suburbs, and branches have been built to the north-east, east and south-east to serve industrial plants. The tram fleet is quite modern, with the last RVZ-6 cars replaced by second-hand Tatras from Germany. A trolleybus line was opened in 1972.

Rolling stock

2030–2044	M4	1972–74	Tatra T4	Ex-Leipzig
2101–2145	M4	1988–89	Tatra T3M	
2201–2252	M4	1987–92	UKVZ KTM-5	
2301–2312	M4	1992–93	UKVZ KTM-8	

This Lipetsk Tatra T4 is the first of a batch received from Leipzig. (A. Olander)

MOSKVA (MOSCOW)   1872   1524mm   185 km

The Russian capital is home to an expanding population that now exceeds 13 million, sprawling 75 km from the central area. The backbone of the public transport system is the metro, which has expanded continuously since the first line was opened in 1935. This, and the large trolleybus system (inaugurated 1933), eliminated tramways from the central area, and further closures have thinned the system as trams remain out of favour in the city government. However there is still an extensive system around the eastern side of the city, with long lines running north and south to feed passengers in to the metro. There is also a detached five-route system in the north-west. The city was always able to secure the best trams for its needs, and more recently any factory trying to build up business has sought to get a demonstration fleet into Moscow. Fleet numbers are prefixed by depot designation digits.

Rolling stock

003–168	M4	1990–94	UKVZ KTM-8
164/9, 221–271	M4	1994–97	UKVZ KTM-17
201–262	M4	1994–99	UKVZ KTM-8M
263–267	M4	2002	UKVZ KTM-19
301–302, 330–342	M4	1999–2002	Tatra T3R
321–326	M4	1990–93	Tatra T7
0130	M4	1998	Lugansk LT-10
0301–0302	M4	1983–84	Tatra T3M
463–996	M4	1982–87	Tatra T3
0003, 2000–48	M4	1998–2002	UKVZ KTM-19
1000	M4	1999	UKVZ KTM-21
1001–1004	M4	2003	Lugansk LT-5
3001	M4	2001	PTMZ LM-2000
3002	M4	2003	PTMZ LM-99
5000–5001	M4	1996	UKVZ KTM-16

Opposite above **Moscow 2001 is one of the KTM-19 trams from Ust Katav factory.** *(Karel Hoorn).*

Opposite below **Advertising liveries are quite common in Moscow, as shown on this T3 serving a suburban housing complex.**

KTM-5 trams were delivered to Naberezhnye-Chelny until 1991.
(A. Olander)

NABEREZHNYE-CHELNY   1973   1524mm   48.4 km

An industrial town on the Kama river, Naberezhnye-Chelny was named Brezhnev from 1982–88 to commemorate its rapid growth during that leadership period, which turned it into the world's largest truck-manufacturing centre. Indeed the tramway was built by and is still operated as a subsidiary of the KAMAZ factory in order to provide transport for its workers from new housing areas. The tramway still has plans for modest extensions, but in the current economic climate progress will be slow.

Rolling stock

001–0131	M4	1983–91	UKVZ KTM-5
0132–0134	M4	1998–2000	UKVZ KTM-8

NIZHNIKAMSK   1967   1524mm   30.1 km

The tramway in this industrial centre, close to Naberezhnye-Chelny, was built by the local petro-chemical combine to serve the needs of its workers, but was municipalised in 1999. Seven routes provide the links between different areas of the town and the industry to the east.

Rolling stock

3–117	M4	1982–87	UKVZ KTM-5
118–125	M4	1997–2002	UKVZ KTM-8

This KTM-5 in Nizhnikamensk is on its way to the NSHZ factory on route 3.
(A. Olander)

NIZHNIY NOVGOROD   1896   1524mm   90.2 km

A major city at the confluence of the Oka and Volga rivers, known as Gorkiy from 1932–1990, Nizhniy Novgorod has a rich history, but was closed to foreigners during the Soviet era. There were two separate tramway systems, with the metre gauge re-gauged in the 1920s to create a unified network. Rapid industrial expansion took place during the Second World War and since, and the busy system has maintained its size despite the opening of metro lines since 1985. However further expansion plans seem to have been dropped, and fleet modernisation is becoming an issue. Trolleybuses began running in 1947.

Rolling stock

1201–1210	M4	1994	UKVZ KTM-8	
1211–1226	M4	1996–98	UKVZ KTM-8M	
1627–1727	M4	1980–87	Tatra T3	
2601–2723	M4	1978–87	Tatra T3	
2805/6	M4	1980	Riga RVZ-6	
2830–2832	M4	1987	Riga RVZ-6	
2901–2932	M4	1988–89	Tatra T3M	2926–32 ex-Ufa
3327–3490	M4	1981–92	UKMZ KTM-5	

The suburbs of Nizhniy Novgorod show that trams offer a smoother ride than motor vehicles.

Noginsk KTM-8M 5 is one of the most modern trams on this one-route system.

NOGINSK   1924   1524mm   10.7 km

Noginsk is a small town with a commuter rail service from Moscow to the south-west. The one route is single track with passing loops and rolling stock and infrastructure problems led to the line being closed in 1992. However repairs took place in 1994 and new rolling stock was obtained to permit the operation to resume, though the level of service is constrained by the track layout.

Rolling stock

1, 2, 4, 5, 11, 36	M4	1995–96	UKVZ KTM-8
3,6	M4	1993	UKVZ KTM-8
7, 9, 10	M4	1980–87	Riga RVZ-6

NOVOCHERKASSK 1954   1524mm   20.2 km

Novocherkassk, in the lower Don industrial region just north of Rostov-na-Donu, has a small four-route tramway which is in need of modernisation, but is unlikely to achieve this in the near future, if ever. The tram fleet is poorly maintained.

Rolling stock

127–159	M4	1982–87	UKVZ KTM-5
201	M4	1994	UKVZ KTM-8

A typical Russian 'tram road' with KTM-5 trams in Novocherkassk.

OREL   1898   1524mm   18 km

An important junction on the railway line from Moscow to Kursk, Orel has a compact central area, but a long tramway line runs west to serve various industrial combines on the other side of the river Oka. The metre-gauge system was regauged in the late 1930s. The undertaking has benefited from operating an all-Tatra fleet. Trolleybuses have been operated since 1968.

Rolling stock

001–085	M4	1979–85	Tatra T3
086–099	M4	1989–90	Tatra T3M

PERM   1929   1524mm   50 km

This is a major industrial city on the Trans-Siberian railway in the western Ural mountains, which grew rapidly after the First World War, requiring the provision of a tramway system. The central area runs east–west along the south bank of the Kama river, and tramway lines run off to various southern suburbs. A new route 5 to Bakharevka has been built in recent years. The tram fleet numbering is complicated by the practice of gap filling, and using even and odd numbers for different batches of trams. The fleet totals around 235 cars. Trolleybus operation dates from 1960.

Rolling stock

001–058	M4	1992–93	UKVZ KTM-8
060–076	M4	1995–99	UKVZ KTM-8M
037/67/9, 116/8/39/64/5/91/2, 254–441	M4	1981–92	UKVZ KTM-5

A coupled set of KTM-8M trams in Perm. (A. Olander)

PYATIGORSK   1903   1000mm   22.5 km

This rather remote town in the north Caucasus was built by the management
of the local mineral water company, and missed out on the extensive regauging
of Soviet systems that took place between the wars. The hilly town is a health
resort, with numerous spas. The main tramway line runs along the valley; there
is a single-track branch north-east to Myascombinat. The odd gauge meant that
the system operated almost wholly Tatra trams, and recent second-hand stock
from Germany has maintained this tradition.

Rolling stock

1–19, 57, 79–119	M4	1974–87	Tatra T3	
11/2/5, 101/2/4/6	M4	1978–83	Tatra T4	Ex-Halle, 5 more expected
120–154	AM4	1988–94	Tatra KT4	
201–212	M4	1995–98	UKVZ KTM-15	

The metre-gauge system at Pyatigorsk has this Tatra KT4 tram. *(A. Olander)*

ROSTOV-NA-DONU   1887   1435mm   49 km

History gave Rostov a Belgian-built (west European) standard-gauge tramway, which grew to such a size that regauging was not economically feasible. Today it is an industrial and port city on the River Don, near the sea of Azov, and also an important cultural centre. There have been some tramway closures in recent years, leaving several sections of track without a passenger service, and track maintenance is to a low standard, but the service has been maintained on the rest of the network by importing second-hand cars from Germany. Trolleybuses have been operated since 1936.

Rolling stock

001–045	M4	1990–95	UKVZ KTM-5	
046–060	M4	1993–94	UKVZ KTM-8	
101–106	M4	1968–71	Tatra T4	Ex-Dresden
308–316	M4	1984–87	Tatra T3	
710–719	M4	1986–87	Tatra T3	
721–726	M4	1969–73	Tatra T4	Ex-Dresden
800–838	M4	1988–89	Tatra T3M	About 25 cars

The tramway workshops at Rostov-na-Donu struggle to keep their Tatra trams supplied with spare parts.

RYAZAN   1963   1524mm   11.6 km

A one-route system built by the NPZ oil refinery, Ryazan's tramway links the historic city on the Oka river with industrial areas to the south. The operation passed to municipal control in about 1999. Trolleybuses have been operated since 1972.

Rolling stock

1–50	M4	1977–92	UKVZ KTM-5	About 30 remain
29, 30, 46, 51–7	M4	1994	UKVZ KTM-8	

SALAVAT   1959   1524mm   17 km

Salavat's one tramway line is served by three routes. The line was built by a local industrial combine, but municipalised in 1971. It links industrial areas to the north with the town centre and residential areas further south. The city has had to drop tramway expansion plans, but has still been able to purchase some new rolling stock to reduce the fleet of RVZ-6 cars.

Rolling stock

2–108	M4	1977–89	Riga RVZ-6
41–3, 001–31	M4	1987–92	UKVZ KTM-5
032–037	M4	1993	UKVZ KTM-8
040, 042–47	M4	1999–2001	UKVZ KTM-8M
038/39/41	M4	1995–99	PTMZ LM-93
048	M4	2002	PTMZ LM-99

SAMARA   1895   1524mm   77.3 km

Samara is an industrial city and Volga river port which was known as Kuybyshev from 1935 until 1991. The wartime capital of the Soviet Union, it is served by an extensive tramway system that has remained intact despite the opening of a metro in 1987. Plans for extensions have however been dropped. The all-Tatra fleet built up in Soviet times has stood the undertaking in good stead, and transfers from Moscow are helping keep up the level of service until new trams can be acquired. Trolleybus operation started in 1942.

Rolling stock

728–898	M4	1973–87	Tatra T3	19 ex-Moskva
854–867	M4	1988	Tatra T3M	
1003–1036	M4	1993	Tatra T3M	
1037	M4	2001	UTM Spektr	
1091–1204	M4	1973–87	Tatra T3	6 ex-Moskva
1205–1206	M4	1998	Tatra T3R	
2002–2174	M4	1975–87	Tatra T3	15 ex-Moskva

Opposite top **Ryazan 30 is one of nine KTM-8 trams in the fleet.** *(A. Olander)*

Opposite centre **The Salavat tramway was built to serve the Urals oil extraction industry and still uses RVZ-6 cars.** *(A. Olander)*

Opposite bottom **Samara operates a large fleet of Tatra T3 trams on its intensive network.** *(A. Olander)*

SANKT PETERBURG (ST PETERSBURG)   1863   1524mm   c.260 km

The world's largest tramway in Russia's second city (Leningrad from 1924–1991) presents a rather sorry picture today, after 12 years of under-investment and political indifference. Rolling stock has fallen into disrepair, and most of the infrastructure is suffering from years of deferred maintenance and poor-quality materials, while the limited public transport funding has been allocated to the metro (first opened in 1955). Traffic has fallen as bus competition has developed and many route closures have taken place, particularly in the central area, though surviving lines often have beautiful restored architecture as a backdrop. In the last years of the Soviet era the system expanded significantly through new housing suburbs in the north and south, on good layouts which survive today. Trams have traditionally been built in the undertaking's workshops, which now trade commercially as PTMZ, but in the 1980s the undertaking had to resort to 'importing' trams built in Ust Katav to meet the need for fleet expansion. Since 1991 new build has been a fraction of what would be required to meet normal fleet turnover, and the fleet has fallen from its nominal level of 1500 cars. Tram numbering includes a depot prefix digit. Trolleybuses have been operated since 1936.

Rolling stock
0301–333, 1423–1634,
1701/5, 2556–2641, 2709/10,
3605–30, 5417–5692,
7468–7646, 8402–8675   M4   1982–88   PTMZ LM-68M
0701–0944   M4   1982–85   UKVZ KTM-5
1001–50, 2215–7, 2401/2,
3001–97, 3201–17/52–75,
3401–58, 5001–5109,
6001–5, 7001–50,
8005–21/35–41, 8113–8208   AM6   1988–98   PTMZ LVS-86
1026–1027   AM6   2002   PTMZ LVS-97
3076   AM8   1990   PTMZ LVS-89
3280   AM8   1994   PTMZ LVS-1–93
3101–4, 3901–2, 5079–91,
6201, 7101–9, 8101–11   AM6   1997–2002   PTMZ LVS-97
0402–29, 0601, 1301–3,
3301–4, 8301–10   M4   2001–03   PTMZ LM-99

This is the locally-built LVS-97 design in St Petersburg.

SARATOV   1887   1524mm   65.3 km

Sprawling along the west bank of the Volga river, Saratov is an industrial city and river port as well as important railway junction and regional centre. The tramway matches the elongated city and includes a light rail line to the north-west to bring workers in from new housing areas. Engels on the east bank of the river is the home of Russia's largest trolleybus factory (they have operated in Saratov since 1952). The standardised tram fleet was all built at Ust-Katav.

Rolling stock

1013–1325	M4	1984–92	UKVZ KTM-5
1326–1328	M4	1996	UKVZ KTM-8M
2034–2086	M4	1984–88	UKVZ KTM-5
2161–2270	M4	1983–90	UKVZ KTM-5
2269/71–85/87	M4	1992–94	UKVZ KTM-8
2286/88	M4	1995	UKVZ KTM-8M

The newest trams in Saratov are this pair of KTM-8M trams, which carry adverts to that effect.
(A. Olander)

Smolensk was the first external customer for the PMTZ LM-99 design of tram.

SMOLENSK   1901   1524mm   27.8 km

An industrial city on the river Dniepr, Smolensk has a long history, though most of the old buildings have been destroyed by the ravages of war over the years. Metre-gauge trams stopped in 1941 and (Russian) standard-gauge trams first ran in 1947. The compact system has closed one of its river-crossing routes in recent years and plans for a new line across the southern suburbs seem to have been abandoned. A trolleybus operation was started in 1991.

Rolling stock

133–205	M4	1988–92	UKVZ KTM-5
206–222	M4	1993–94	UKVZ KTM-8
223–226	M4	1995–97	UKVZ KTM-8M
227–230	M4	1988–89	PTMZ LM-93
231–232	M4	2001	PTMZ LM-99
233	M4	2001	UKVZ KTM-8M

Russia's newest tramway was built in Stary Oskol. This KTM-5 set is unusually using the photograph on the rear car. *(A. Olander)*

Below **Taganrog** on the Lower Don has a fleet of KTM-5 trams.

STARIY OSKOL   1980   1524mm   26.1 km

Stariy Oskol is near Russia's border with the Ukraine. The long north–south tramway was built as a light rail line by the local electro-metallurgical industry to improve transport between various factories and residential areas. The original rolling stock has been boosted by some newer cars, but trackwork is suffering from deferred maintenance.

Rolling stock

6–95	M4	1977–83	UKVZ KTM-5
96	M4	2001	UKVZ KTM-19

TAGANROG   1932   1524mm   22.8 km

An industrial city, Azov sea port and railway junction in the lower Don region, Taganrog lies just west of Rostov. The tramway links the two railway stations with local factories. A standard tram fleet is maintained in reasonable condition. Trolleybuses have been operated since 1977.

Rolling stock

260–342	M4	1981–89	UKVZ KTM-5
346–351	M4	1993–94	UKVZ KTM-8

TULA   1888   1524mm   43.2 km

190 km south of Moscow, Tula is known for its armaments factories, but is a more general industrial centre with steel and chemical plants. This means the tramway system is a busy one with a good level of service relative to its size. The Russian standard gauge operation dates from 1927. Single-track route 4 runs south across country to Kosaya Gora. The undertaking has maintained its Tatra fleet at a high level by buying withdrawn cars from Moscow. Trolleybus operation started in 1962.

Rolling stock

1–149	M4	1976–87	Tatra T3	Many ex-Moskva
13/14/17/18, 23–30.				
47/8, 55/6, 83/4	M4	1989–96	Tatra T3M	
21/22, 69/70, 115	M4	1993	UKVZ KTM-8	
201–268	M4	1979–86	Tatra T3	Many ex-Moskva
300–358	M4	1988–89	Tatra T3M	
401–442	M4	1981–86	Tatra T3	Some ex-Moskva

Tula was one of the last systems to receive new Tatra T3M trams before the break-up of the Soviet Union. *(A. Olander)*

TVER   1901   1524mm   39 km

This industrial city and river port on the Volga was known as Kalinin from 1931–1990. 160 km north-west of Moscow, a tramway has been built across a second river bridge in recent years. The system serves all parts of the city with a good level of service. Tatra trams have been supplemented by deliveries from Ust Katav. The first trolleybus ran in 1967.

Rolling stock

1–38, 136/8	M4	1985–88	Tatra T3M
5, 7, 8, 10	M4	1980–81	Tatra T3
63/75/9/82/90/5	M4	1977	Tatra T3
103–135/7/9/41	M4	1978–81	Tatra T3
140/2–170	M4	1992–93	UKVZ KTM-8
241–257	M4	1991–92	UKVZ KTM-5
259–274	M4	1993	UKVZ KTM-8

One of the few Russian systems to try adopting a new livery is Tver. *(A. Olander)*

This KTM-19 tram in Ufa shows the latest development in UKVZ design.

UFA 1937 1524mm 60.9 km

The capital of Bashkria, on the western fringe of the Ural mountains, Ufa is on a traditional trade route and the river Belaya. Its tramway serves the compact old centre with a loop and branches, and links north to a second system serving industry and modern housing areas. A planned extension has been cancelled for financial reasons, but service levels have been maintained by buying second-hand Tatras from Germany. The varied tram fleet has cars from all Russian factories. Trolleybus operation opened in 1962.

Rolling stock

1004–1005	M4	1995		PTMZ LM-93
1009/12, 2001–5	M4	1995–6	UKVZ	KTM-8M
1025–1113	M4	1983–87		Riga RVZ-6
1114–1164	M4	1992–93		UKVZ KTM-8
1165–1167	M4	1991–92		UKVZ KTM-5
2006–17/34–39	M4	1993		UKVZ KTM-8
2019–2033	M4	1991–92		UKVZ KTM-5
2018	M4	1999		UKVZ KTM-19
2046	M4	2001		UTM Spektr
2501	M4	1993		UKVZ KTM-8
2020–47, 3005–31, 3091, 3136–43	M4	1970–74		Tatra T3 31 ex-Chemnitz
2040, 3001–3175	M4	1978–87		Tatra T3

Ulyanovsk maintained a wholly Tatra fleet until 1991. *(A. Olander)*

ULYANOVSK   1954   1524mm   59.3 km

This hilltop city overlooking the Volga river has a funicular down to the river bank. In addition to being Lenin's birthplace, it is an industrial city with a dense tramway network. Two lines have been extended recently, using single track for reasons of economy, serving western and north-western suburbs. A Tatra-only fleet through the 1970s and 80s, the products of Russian factories have since been tried, but withdrawn trams from Moscow have also been acquired. Trolleybuses have been operated since 1973.

Rolling stock

1088–1195	M4	1974–86	Tatra T3	
1198–1209	M4	1991	UKVZ KTM-5	
1210–1213	M4	1994	UKVZ KTM-8	
1214–1215	M4	1995	UKVZ KTM-8M	
1220–1221	M4	1996	PTMZ LM-93	
1216–1234, 2045/6	M4	1976–82	Tatra T3	Ex-Moskva
2049–2162	M4	1973–86	Tatra T3	
2163–72, 2218–31	M4	1982–87	Tatra T3	Ex-Moskva
2179–2217	M4	1988–91	Tatra T3M	

UST KATAV   1973   1524 mm   2 km

Ust Katav is a town in the Ural mountains which has had a rolling stock factory beside the hydro-electric plant underneath the Katav dam since 1899. Trams have been built here at various times, but under the planned Soviet economy the factory has assumed major responsibility for tramcar production since 1947. From 1969 until 1991 about 14,500 trams were built here (650 per year), since then only some 1500 (125 per year). The works test track, which includes sharp curves and steep gradients, was built through housing areas, and carried passengers at peak periods for several years, although not at present.

Vladikavkaz has purchased second-hand trams from Germany since 1996. This Tatra T4 ran in Leipzig. *(S. Spengler)*

VLADIKAVKAZ   1904   1524mm   27.8 km

This city is the capital of the North Ossetian Republic in the Caucasus mountains, bordering Chechnya, and is an important military and political centre. It was named Ordzhonikidze from 1931–1990. The metre-gauge tramway was regauged in the mid-1930s and serves housing and industrial areas on each side of the river Terek. A suburban extension to routes 1/4 has been built recently. The tram fleet has been boosted by the arrival of second-hand Tatras from Germany. Trolleybuses have been operated since 1977.

Rolling stock

107–108	M4	1981	Tatra T3	
112, 114	M4	1988	Tatra T3M	
145–149	M4	1991	UKVZ KTM-5	
150–170	M4	1993	UKVZ KTM-8	
171–180	M4	1973–75	Tatra T4	Ex-Leipzig
181–193	M4	1979–81	Tatra T3	Ex-Schwerin
194–206	M4	1969–70	Tatra T3	Ex-Chemnitz
207–222	M4	1975–81	Tatra T4	Ex-Dresden

Volgograd's light rail line is operated by coupled sets of Tatra trams.

VOLGOGRAD   1913   1524mm   61.8 km

Volgograd is more famous as Stalingrad, a name it carried from 1925–61. This major city on the Volga river was almost destroyed in World War Two, but has been rebuilt and is now an industrial centre and inland port. The tramway system is quite compact for the size of the city, and includes a light rail line to the north that runs in subway in the central area and has no track connection with the rest of the system. Also separated is the one route in the formerly independent town of Krasnoarmeisk, to the south, which was opened to serve the oil refinery there in 1958. Ust Katav built a special double-ended twin-set to serve the light rail line, but coupled Tatra sets are preferred instead. A further subway extension south has been partly built for several years, but remains to be completed. A trolleybus network has been built up since 1960.

Rolling stock

2456–2741	M4	1969–82	Tatra T3
2834–2853	M4	1987–90	Tatra T3M
2854–2855	M4	1992	UKVZ KTM-11
3001–3043	M4	1971–86	Tatra T3
5463/68/70	M4	1976	Tatra T3
5699–5833	M4	1978–87	Tatra T3
5834	AM8	1984	Tatra KT8
5835	AM8	1995	PTMZ LVS-2-93

VOLZHSKIY   1963   1524mm   31 km

This small town is almost a north-east suburb of Volgograd, and the tramway was built and operated by the textile combine that employs much of the town's workforce. It was municipalised in 1987. Six routes are operated, mostly on reserved track.

Rolling stock

62–136	M4	1975–81	Tatra T3	40 cars
137–171	M4	1988–91	UKVZ KTM-5	

VORONEZH   1891   1524mm   c.60 km

Voronezh is an industrial city on the river of the same name, some 450 km south of Moscow. Its Belgian-built metre-gauge tramway was abandoned in 1919 and the Russian-gauge electric tramway opened in 1926. The tramway system provided a quite dense network of routes until 2002, when there were significant closures, including two of the three depots. The Tatra fleet of 160 trams was withdrawn at this time, including second-hand cars acquired from Germany in 1996–99. The future of the remaining system is uncertain. Trolleybuses have been operated since 1960.

Rolling stock

300–404	M4	1986–90	UKVZ KTM-5

It is believed that use of Tatra trams in Voronezh has now ceased. *(A. Olander)*

Yaroslavl has a complete fleet of Ust-Katav built trams. *(A. Olander)*

YAROSLAVL   1900   1524mm   29.9 km

An industrial and river port city on the Volga river, 240 km north-east of Moscow, Yaroslavl has many old buildings, and is a well-known textile centre. Its tramway serves the railway station, city centre, industrial plants and housing areas. A high level of service is provided by the 150-car fleet, where gap-filling of fleet numbers is practised. Trolleybus operation started in 1949.

Rolling stock

2–211	M4	1985–91	UKVZ KTM-5
20, 34–36	M4	1993	UKVZ KTM-8
83–85	M4	1992	UKVZ KTM-8
100	M4	2000	UKVZ KTM-19
139/40/5/6	M4	1992–93	UKVZ KTM-8

ZLATOUST   1934   1524 mm   22.5 km

Alphabetically the last tramway city in Russia, Zlatoust in the Ural mountains is also the last tramway city in Europe as it turns into Asia. Well-known for steel products such as cutlery and engraved items, its two-route tramway runs into the surrounding hills to reach quite rural scenery. Gap filling of fleet numbers is practised.

Rolling stock

2–111	M4	1980–92	UKVZ KTM-5	about 55 cars
112–117	M4	1992–93	UKVZ KTM-8	
1–127	M4	1995–2000	UKVZ KTM-8M	18 cars

Zlatoust in the Urals is Europe's most easterly tramway. *(A. Olander)*

Beograd is now refurbishing is fleet of Tatra KT4 trams.

SERBIA

After the break-up of the former Yugoslav Republic, Serbian and Montenegro retained the name of this entity. However they now function as *de facto* states, and the Serb capital Belgrade is the only city with a tramway system.

BEOGRAD (BELGRADE)   1886   1000mm   60 km

The capital of the former Yugoslavia is an historic city at the confluence of the Danube and Sava rivers, but there are relatively few old buildings in the city centre and much new housing in the expanding suburbs. The tramway has six lines radiating from a central area circular route. There is traditional street track, including some gutter running, but much reservation on newer routes to the south and west. Tatra trams from Czechoslovakia were used to create a modern tram fleet, but economic sanctions and the effects of the war brought the system to a very poor state. Now life has returned to normal and, while the Tatra fleet is being refurbished, Switzerland has donated a batch of Basel articulated trams and trailers to boost services.

Rolling stock

201–400	AM4	1980–90	Tatra KT4	
401–420	AM4	1997	Tatra KT4	
456	M4	1958	Schindler	Ex-Basel
603–22	AM6	1967	Duewag	Ex-Basel
625/30–240/57	AM6	1972	Duewag	Ex-Basel
1004	M4	1976	Tatra T4	Ex-Halle, not in service
1335–40/2–4	B3	1957–64	BVB/SLM	Ex-Basel
1401/5/7/9–13/5	B4	1947–48	FFA	Ex-Basel
341–343	B4	1961	FFA	Ex-Basel via Bern

SLOVAKIA

The rump state of the former Czechoslovakia has faced considerable economic difficulties, and proposals for an automatic mini-metro in Bratislava were abandoned, while tramway development has come to a halt. However Slovakia should benefit from its accession to the EU.

BRATISLAVA   1895   1000mm   36.7 km

The capital of Slovakia is an attractive city on the river Danube, with a well-preserved central area. The street tramways here extend out on reservation to new housing areas in the north. Trams on the western route use a dedicated tram tunnel under Bratislava Castle. Further extensions and plans to convert to standard gauge have been on hold due to economic problems. The Tatra tram fleet is slowly being modernised, pending the ability to buy new stock.

Rolling stock

7053–7087	AM6	1969–77	Tatra K2
7101–7109	AM6	1998–2000	Pars Sumperk (rebuilt Tatras)
7301–7303	M4	1998–2000	Pars Sumperk (rebuilt Tatras)
7602/7/10	M4	1966	Tatra T3
7701–7846	M4	1976–89	Tatra T3
7901–7956	M4	1991–1998	Tatra T6

KOSICE   1891   1435mm   33.6 km

This provincial town in eastern Slovakia has an attractive centre, with street track, surrounded by old and new housing areas, where tramways have been extended on reservation. A long cross-country line built in 1964 runs on private right-of-way south to the VSZ steel works, but has a very limited service except in connection with shift changes, and the original high-speed service has degraded as infrastructure becomes overdue for renewal. After standardising on Tatra bogie trams, some new articulated cars were purchased, but some were since sold to other systems to raise funds. In the summer a horse tram service is operated on new tram track in the central precinct.

Rolling stock

229/98/301/2	M4	1976–79	Tatra T3
322–424	M4	1966–89	Tatra T3
500–517	AM8	1986–87	Tatra KT8
600–628	M4	1991–3	Tatra T6

Other lines

The 35-km metre-gauge TEZ electric light railway links the rail station at Poprad Tatry with the High Tatras mountain resorts of Tatranska Lomnica, Stary Smokovec and Strbske Pleso. 18 three section Tatra-built articulated cars have been mostly replaced by new low-floor stock from Stadler. At Strbske Pleso there is a Swiss-style rack tramway down to the railway station at Strba.

A 5.4-km 760-mm gauge roadside interurban tramway links the railway station at Trencianska Tepla with the spa town of Trencianske Teplice. Passenger service is provided by three bogie cars and two trailers, and the line was recently refurbished after a period of closure.

The metre-gauge Bratislava system features modern track layouts.

The segregated high-speed line to the steel works south of Kosice operates three-car sets for shift changes.

The modified LRVs on Istanbul's tramway are about to be replaced by new low-floor cars.

TURKEY

For long a country without tramways, Turkey has in recent years built several new systems ranging from street trams to light rail and pre-metro. Most of these are in Asiatic Turkey (Adana, Ankara, Antalya, Bursa, Konya, Izmir), but the country's largest city, Istanbul, has a variety of operations on the European side.

ISTANBUL   1989   1435mm   28.2 km

This great Turkish city athwart the Bosphorus, once known as Constantinople, opened a new light rail line in 1989, to link Aksaray on the western edge of the old city with a large suburban bus interchange. This segregated high-platform line has been extended in stages south-west to the airport. Rolling stock consists of three-car trains of Swedish-built articulated cars. In 1992 a street tramway was built to link Sirkeci station on the Golden Horn with Aksaray, since extended to Topkapi bus station. Initially some of the Swedish LRVs were fitted with skirts to operate the tramway (which had high platforms built in the street). Now delivery is in progress of 55 low-floor trams that will take over the tramway operation, releasing the original cars for improved light rail service. There is also a heritage tramway with museum cars operating between Taksim and Tunel along a pedestrianised street in the new town. Further tramways are at the planning stage.

Rolling stock

101–135	AM6	1988/89	ASEA	No driving positions
501–570	AM6	1988/89	ASEA	22 adapted for street operation
(55)	AM6	2002–03	Bombardier	Low floor

Avdiyivka's tramway line links housing areas such as this with industrial combines.

UKRAINE

The Ukraine formed a substantial part of the former Soviet Union, and since independence in 1991 has forged ahead economically, although many older traditional industries have declined. Substantial numbers of Russians still live within its borders, particularly in the Crimea. Ukraine still uses the Cyrillic alphabet, although pronunciation varies from Russian, resulting in differing transliteration of city names. No tramways have been closed in the Ukraine since independence, but public transport investment has been low on the list of priorities, and far fewer newer trams have been delivered than is required to maintain the average age of the fleet. Routine infrastructure maintenance has also been neglected on many systems.

AVDIYIVKA   1965   1524mm   15.5 km
This town lies just north of the Donets'k city limits and grew up around the giant coke-chemical combine. This was responsible for the construction and operation of the single line through to today. The southern section was closed in 2000, and the remaining tramway is wholly on reserved track. Just three trams are used off-peak, but up to 15 at shift change times.

Rolling stock
030–064   M4   1978–91   UKVZ KTM-5   28 cars

DNIPRODZERZHINSK 1935   1524mm   43 km

Built on the banks of the river Dnipr. Dniprodzerzhinsk had plans for a river-crossing light rail line, but these have had to be abandoned due to the economic situation. The compact system links residential and industrial areas, and some efforts have been made to modernise the tram fleet.

Rolling stock

101/6–8/10/4/5/9/20	M4	1993	UKVZ KTM-8
104, 1015/6/21/36/46/50/5/6	M4	1989	UKVZ KTM-8
121–127	M4	1996–97	UKVZ KTM-8M
645–688	M4	1981–87	Tatra T3
2000–2004	M4	1996–2000	Tatra-Yug T3M

DNIPROPETROVSK 1897   1524mm   88 km

This industrial port city on the Dnipr river maintains a large tramway system, despite the opening of a metro line in 1981. Trams cross two river bridges to serve different parts of the northern suburbs, and there are complicated single-track street loops in the central area. When Tatra fleet deliveries ceased the undertaking turned to Ust Katav for its trams, but is now trying the locally-built Tatra-Jug design. Trolleybus operation started in 1947.

Rolling stock

1077/8/82, 1120/3	M4	1971–2	Tatra T3
1160/61/63/69	M4	1974	Tatra T3
1181–1378	M4	1976–87	Tatra T3
1500–1520	M4	1991	UKVZ KTM-5
2118–2212	M4	1983–91	UKVZ KTM-5
2210/13–18	M4	1991–94	UKVZ KTM-8
2219–2242	M4	1995–96	UKVZ KTM-8M
3001–3012	M4	1996–2002	Tatra-Jug T3M

DONET'SK   1928   1524mm   65 km

The capital of the Donbass industrial region, Donet'sk has maintained a good public transport service through regulation, and despite its industrial nature has also made some attempt on environmental improvements. It was known as Stalino from 1924 to 1961. High-frequency trunk tram routes link the central area with hilly suburbs. The undertaking has maintained a wholly-Tatra fleet. Depot prefix digits are used. Trolleybuses have been operated since 1940.

Rolling stock

102–181	M4	1972–87	Tatra T3	
708–806	M4	1967–75	Tatra T3	
808–814	M4	1972–73	Tatra T3	Ex-Dniprodzerzhinsk
901–963	M4	1975–84	Tatra T3	
3001–3006	M4	2003	Tatra-Yug T3M	

A works tram for watering the streets of Dniprodzerzhinsk with Tatras in the background.

The Dnipr river bridge carries Dnipropetrovsk tram routes 6 and 9 to the north side.

A clutch of Tatra trams meet in the centre of Donet'sk.

The tramway is an important part of community life in Druzhkivka.

DRUZHKIVKA   1945   1524mm   13 km

A small town in the Donbass industrial region, with an engineering industry base, the tramway here also has some semi-rural sections serving low-density housing areas. The line to the railway station is single track with passing loops. A standard tram fleet is operated.

Rolling stock
053–089   M4   1976–86   UKVZ KTM-5

HORLIVKA   1932   1524mm   31 km

This industrial Donbass town has fallen on hard times with local plant closures and service frequencies are low, although no sections have been abandoned yet. There is a street loop around the central area and a long route 8 running east through village-type communities. With no new trams for 13 years, fleet maintenance is a problem. Trolleybuses were introduced in 1974.

Rolling stock
374–424   M4   1980–90   UKVZ KTM-5

Tramways serve the Horlivka mines in the Donbass region.

KHARKIV   1882   1524mm   125 km

Kharkiv is the second-largest city in the Ukraine and has maintained its tramway system as the fourth-largest in the former Soviet Union, despite the arrival of a metro in 1975 (this has resulted in just one tram line closure). It is an industrial centre and market city, as well as an important railway centre. Tatra trams are much-favoured here, and the small fleet of KTM-5 cars was withdrawn in 2002. The traditional route network serves all areas of the city. Trolleybuses have operated since 1939.

Rolling stock

219–774	M4	1973–86	Tatra T3	
1507/8/11–8	M4	1986/7	Tatra T3	
1700/34–1899	M4	1978–85	Tatra T3	
1519–1573	M4	1988–91	Tatra T3M	30 cars
3001–3064	M4	1980–87	Tatra T3	
7000	M4	1978	Tatra T3	

The extensive Kharkiv tramway system serves the busy central area.

New and older Tatra trams on street track in Kiev.

KYIV (KIEV)   1892   1524mm   130 km

The Ukranian capital is a hilly city beside the Dnipr river with much new housing on the east bank. The large tramway system has been much reduced in size over recent years as the metro, first opened in 1960, has expanded, but new tramway construction is still taking place on the east bank, and there is also a light rail line linking the main railway station with south-west suburbs. One river bridge used by trams links the two parts of the system. The tram fleet has been rationalised to concentrate on Tatra cars. A large trolleybus system has been built up since 1935.

Rolling stock

002–077	M4	1985–90	Tatra T3M
100/1, K-1	M4	1994, 2001	Tatra-Yug T3M
301–318	M4	1988	Tatra T3M
5185–5194	M4	1970	Tatra T3
5319–5688	M4	1966–86	Tatra T3
5701–5858	M4	1978–85	Tatra T3
5901–6032	M4	1979–86	Tatra T3

Konotop operates only UKVZ KTM-5 trams.

KONOTOP   1949   1524mm   21 km

This small town in the northern Ukraine has an interesting tramway system with two 'mini' systems linked by a double-track trunk line. Each part of the system features single-track lines with passing loops, and service frequencies are rather low. No new trams have arrived since 1989, and fleet maintenance of the 30 cars is a problem.

Rolling stock

45–98	M4	1975–89	UKVZ KTM-5	
99–101	M4	1983	UKVZ KTM-5	Ex-Dnepropetrovsk

KOSTYATINIVKA   1931   1524mm   25.5 km

This Donbass town north of Donet'sk is a centre for heavy industry, but outside the industrial areas the tramway serves pleasant hilly suburbs with low-rise housing developments. Route 3 to the west is single-track with passing loops. The tram fleet is well-maintained and a rare feature is staff uniforms.

Rolling stock

117–167	M4	1977–90	UKVZ KTM-5

Kostyantinivka route 3 climbs on single track high above industrial districts.

Modern housing provides the backdrop to this KTM-5 in Kramatorsk.

KRAMATORSK   1937   1524mm   19 km

A small Donbass industrial town, the three-route tramway runs extra services for shift changes at industrial plants, and operates in a fashion unchanged for many years. The fleet is not well-maintained, despite some attempts at cosmetic paint jobs. Trolleybuses began operating in 1971.

Rolling stock
0004–0059   M4   1973–91   UKVZ KTM-5

The light rail line in Kriviy Rig adopts left-hand running in order to serve island platforms.

KRIVIY RIH   1935   1524mm   60 km

This city in the Donets basin of the southern Ukraine was just a village until iron ore was discovered, but is now one of the world's biggest iron and uranium mining centres. In addition to the main system a new light rail line to the north-east was opened in 1986–99, and this features some subway sections. Ust Katav developed a new design of tramway triple-sets with double-sided but single-ended cars operating back-to-back with motorised trailers for this line, but coupled Tatra sets are preferred by the undertaking, and second-hand examples have been sought throughout eastern Europe. 1957 saw the inauguration of trolleybus operation.

Rolling stock

001–050	M4	1986–87	Tatra T3	
051/2	M4	1987	Tatra T3	Ex-Zaporozhye
053–063	M4	1963–70	Tatra T3	Ex-Praha (Prague)
329–459/77/8	M4	1978–92	UKVZ KTM-5	
460–463	M4	1992/3	UKVZ KTM-8	
464–476	M4	1995–97	UKVZ KTM-8M	
201–3/5/6/8/9/11	M4	1993–95	UKVZ KTM-11	
204/7/10	B4	1994–95	UKVZ KTM-11P	

LUGAN'SK   1934   1524mm   46 km

The easternmost of the Donbass tramways is 30 km from the Russian border, and the city was known as Voroshilovgrad in Soviet times. Coal mines are all around and local industry includes a railway rolling stock factory that decided to diversify into tramcar production, without much success. The system has more street tramway than many former Soviet systems, with high peak frequencies, but off-peak service can be sparse. Trolleybuses started running in 1962.

Rolling stock
095–192	M4	1976–91	UKVZ KTM-5
202–208	M4	1994–98	Lugan'sk LT-10

This locally-built LT-10 tram climbs high above Lugan'sk on route 6.

Coupled metre-gauge KT4 trams in the historic centre of L'viv.

L'VIV   1880   1000mm   33.5 km

This attractive city from the Austro-Hungarian empire was part of Poland until 1939, and has many old buildings in the central area. The tramway system includes a city circle, street track and suburban branches to industrial and housing areas. The Tatra fleet reflects the metre-gauge requirements of the system. Trolleybuses have operated since 1952.

Rolling stock

802–873	M4	1973–79	Tatra T4	
874–883	M4	1973–76	Tatra T4	Ex-Kaliningrad
1001–1145	AM4	1976–88	Tatra KT4	

MAKIYIVKA   1925   1524mm   31.5 km

A steel town, just outside Donet'sk in the Donbass basin, local industry has declined and the tramway system, which was built and operated by the coal combine before municipalisation in 2001, is in a poor state. Sometimes just four trams from the nominal serviceable stock of 15 are operated. However it seems some efforts to improve things are underway, with second-hand trams being refurbished in Donet'sk for the undertaking. Trolleybuses began in 1979.

Rolling stock

170–247	M4	1980–91	UKVZ KTM-5	244–7 second-hand

A newly-repainted KTM-5 in Makiyivka passes the defunct steelworks.

Tram passengers in Mariupol have little road traffic to worry about.

MARIUPOL   1933   1524mm   56 km

A port city on the north shore of the Sea of Azov, Mariupol was known as Zhadanov from 1948 to 1989. The tramway system features loop routes with different route numbers used in each direction. The tram fleet is rather old and maintenance is a problem. Trolleybus operation dates from 1970.

Rolling stock

400–409/12	M4	1982–91	UKVZ KTM-5
410/11, 601–603	M4	1994	UKVZ KTM-8
501–505	M4	1982–88	UKVZ KTM-5
733–978	M4	1976–91	UKVZ KTM-5

MIKOLAYIV   1887   1524mm   36.5 km

This Black Sea port 110 km north-east of Odesa is a shipbuilding centre and naval base. The tramway system mostly serves wide east–west streets and still has plans for expansion to create another north–south link. The undertaking has been modernising its fleet with Tatra-Jug trams. Trolleybuses began operating in 1967.

Rolling stock

1039–1096	M4	1979–89	UKVZ KTM-5
1915	M4	2001	Tatra-Jug T3M
2001–2002	M4	2000–01	Tatra-Jug T3M
2025–2125	M4	1980–92	UKVZ KTM-5
2126–2132	M4	1994	UKVZ KTM-8

This Tatra-Jug in Mikolayiv is a locally produced version of the Czech T3M.

The summer-only Molochnoye tramway serves a workers' rest home on the Crimean coast.

MOLOCHNOYE   1990   1000mm   1.5 km

This single-track tramway with no intermediate loop was built by a sanatorium on the Crimean coast to carry residents across flat marshes to reach the beach for bathing. Yevpatoria supplied a couple of Gotha trams which are operated back-to-back. The service operates only during the summer (late May to mid-September).

Rolling stock

5	M2	1958	Gotha T57	ex-Yevpatoria
20	M2	1960	Gotha T59	ex-Yevpatoria

The latest livery is seen on this Tatra T3 in the centre of Odesa.

ODESA   1910   1524mm   110 km

A sea port and tourist resort on the Black Sea coast, Odesa stands on a group
of hills and boasts many attractive buildings and a rich cultural life. The compact tramway system is concentrated in the central area, with much street track,
and long suburban extensions to the north and the south (the latter route 19
with single track at the outer end). Metre-gauge operation ceased in 1971,
although regauging started in 1934. The all-Tatra tram fleet has been boosted
with some second-hand examples. Trolleybuses have been operated since 1945.

Rolling stock

1019/20/21	M4	1974	Tatra T3	Ex-Mariupol
1038–1049	M4	1970–75	Tatra T3	Ex-Moskva
2945–3339	M4	1970–87	Tatra T3	
4001–4089	M4	1983–85	Tatra T3	
5001–5020	M4	1980–87	Tatra T3	Ex-Moskva
7001	M4	2001	Tatra-Jug T3M	

The short tramway in Stakhanov includes this railway crossing near the central market.

STAKHANOV   1937   1524mm   9.5 km

This old industrial town in the Donbass was named Kadiyevka until 1978. It is now in decline and two of the three tramway routes have been closed leaving just a line from the centre north-east to Teplogorsk (with single track at the outer end). Only two trams operate off-peak, with service doubled in the morning peak. The future of the system is uncertain. The town has operated trolleybuses since 1970.

Rolling stock
084–091   M4   1988–89   UKVZ KTM-5

VINNITSYA   1913   1000mm   20 km

A city 190 km south-west of Kiev in the centre of rich farmland, Vinnitsa is dominated by agricultural-based industries. The tramway runs from the railway station through the city centre before splitting into three lines. An alternative link from the centre to the west has long been planned but seems unlikely to materialise. The metre-gauge guaranteed a supply of Tatra trams to the undertaking, and these are maintained in fair condition. Trolleybus operation started in 1964.

Rolling stock
110–147   M4   1971–79   Tatra T4
149–228   AM4   1981–90   Tatra KT4

The tramway junction in the centre of Vinnitsya brings all five routes together.

A well-filled KTM-5
runs through indus-
trial areas of
Yenakiyevo.

YENAKIYEVE   1932   1524mm   16.5 km

This old industrial town in the Donbass is now a depressed area. The tramway, which features a town centre street-based loop, is in poor condition and trams operate in a deplorable state, with only about 20 of the 40 cars in use.

Rolling stock

001–055	M4	1976–90	UKMZ KTM-5	
043–045	M4	1975–76	UKMZ KTM-5	Ex-Mariupol
Y1–Y2	M4	1978	UKMZ KTM-5	

YEVPATORIYA   1914   1000MM   18 KM

This seaport and tourist resort on the west coast of the Crimea has an old Turkish quarter in the town centre and splendid beaches. The tramway is all single track with passing loops (apart from one suburban extension) and is the last place in the former Soviet Union to operate two-axle trams in town service and with trailers. Track and rolling stock are not in good condition.

Rolling stock

7, 9, 10, 12	M2	1958–60	Gotha T57	7/12 ex-Simferopol 9/10 ex-Zwickau
3, 11, 14, 18, 19	M2	1958–60	Gotha T57	3/11/4 ex-Simferopol
51–53, 62, 63	B2	1958–60	Gotha B57	53/62/3 ex-Simferopol
30–47	AM4	1987–90	Tatra KT4	

ZAPORIZHYA   1932   1524mm   55 km

An industrial city on the river Dnipr, nearby dams provide hydro-electric power for the city's metal and machinery industries. The tramway provides most local public transport needs, with a reasonable service level on a traditional network. The undertaking has retained its preference for Tatra trams. Trolleybuses first ran in 1949.

Rolling stock

274–399	M4	1968–87	Tatra T3	
416–458	M4	1988–94	Tatra T3M	
459–466	M4	1995–96	Tatra-Jug T3M	
550–576, 695	M4	1977–78	Tatra T3	Ex-Dniprodzerzhinsk
700–809	M4	1979–87	Tatra T3	

Yevpatoriya features two-axle trams and single-track and loop layouts.

Coupled Tatra T3M trams operate on route 1 in Zaporizhya.

The small town of Zhitomir gets a good service from its Tatra-equipped tramway.

ZHITOMIR   1899   1000mm   9 km

This city 130 km west of Kyiv is in the centre of a hop-growing district and is noted for brewing and other agricultural industries. The single route 5 is the survivor of a larger system, most of which was replaced by trolleybuses in the 1960s, but is set to be retained for as long as its Tatra trams can be maintained.

Rolling stock
| 1–18 | M4 | 1977–79 | Tatra T4 |
| 19–38 | AM4 | 1981–88 | Tatra KT4 |

BIBLIOGRAPHY

To keep this book up to date you need to read:
Tramways & Urban Transit (monthly) published by the Light Rail Transit Association, PO Box 302, Gloucester, GL4 4ZD (www.lrta.org)
Blickpunkt Strassenbahn (bi-monthly) published Arbeitsgemeinschaft Blickpunkt Stassenbahn, Burgherrenstr 2, D-12101 Berlin (www.blickpunktstrab.net).
Tramway Atlas of the former Soviet Union, published 2003 by Arbeitsgemeinschaft Blickpunkt Strassenbahn in conjunction with LRTA and available in the UK from LRTA (see above).